Warman's®
Coca-Cola®
Collectibles

Play *refreshed*... have a Coke

Allan Petretti

Identification and Price Guide

©2006 Allan Petretti
Published by

kp books
An Imprint of F+W Publications

700 East State Street • Iola, WI 54990-0001
715-445-2214 • 888-457-2873

Our toll-free number to place an order or obtain
a free catalog is (800) 258-0929.

Library of Congress Catalog Number: 2005931488

ISBN-13: 978-0-89689-311-5
ISBN-10: 0-89689-311-1

Designed by Donna Mummery
Edited by Dan Brownell

Printed in China

Dedication

To my wonderful wife, Rannie, and my three great children, Dante, Deanna, and Vito, who have shared their husband and father with Coca-Cola for all these years...I love you all.

Acknowledgments

Thank you to all the people below, all of whom I consider friends. Without their generous contribution of time, knowledge, and materials, this book would not have been possible.

Fred Dobbs
Susan Anievas
Don & Donna Arnold
Dave Baker
Greg Barney, Sr.
Richard Bostwick
Jeff Brady
Gordon Breslow
Freddy Brewer
Dr. & Mrs. Eugene Brinker
Don Brunjes
Chuck Campbell
Joe Davis
Larry Dikeman
Fred Dobbs
Robert & Audrey Flinn
Dave Goddard
Bert Hansen
Sharon & Joe Happle
Chuck Hardy
Bill & Kay Hendricks
Randy Inman
Jerry Jacobs
Vincent Jacono
James D. Julia, Inc.

Jack Kelly
Darryl Kirbo
Thaddeous Krom
Rudy LeCoadic
Harper Lieper
Fred Maney
Blaine Martin
James McDonald
Gary Metz
Jay & Joan Millman
Robert Morawic
John Morgerson
Bob Nance
Robert Nelson
Billy Osborne
Ted Oswalt
Ron Paradoski
Phil Perdue
Robert Rentzer
Scott Rosenman
Bill & Jan Schmidt
Larry Schulz
Neal Selznick
Irv & Dot Shirley
John Wise

Larry & Nancy Werner
Bill Whitaker
Jeff Wright

With Special Thanks To . . .
John Barbier
Bill Bateman
Marc Cardelli
The Coca-Cola Company/Phillip F. Mooney, Archives Manager
Gael & Rosalie deCourtivron
Jim Meehan
Bob Newman
Dann & Jinx Perszyk
Pop Poppenheimer (1922–1988)
Danny Ragsdale
Rodger Robinson
Randy Schaeffer
Leonard J. and Joseph L. Schiff
Thom & Frances Thompson
Don & Marty Weinberger
Alan Wright
John Yarbrough

Contents

Introduction

Public fascination with Coca-Cola goes far beyond the fact that it has been America's number one soft drink since its humble beginnings in 1886. The truth is that its success is based on more than great taste and high quality. That kind of longevity and success requires a combination of excellent product, good business practices, loyal employees and the foresight to make advertising a top priority. Coca-Cola's advertising is what this book is all about. Fortunately, items are available at all price levels, so virtually anyone can collect them.

Scope of this Book

This book, as well as my exhaustive reference book, *Petretti's Coca-Cola Collectibes Price Guide*, only deals with original, true "vintage" Coca-Cola advertising and production material, and has a cut-off date set in the early 1970s.

New, commemorative, and made-for-the-collector-market items aren't listed, as they comprise an entirely different market. I also don't list vending machines, because many fine books about these machines have been written by authors far more knowledgeable in that area than me.

Pricing

The values in this book are not assigned arbitrarily. Years of tracking this memorabilia, supported by a program of consistent and thorough research, provide the basis for evaluating each and every piece shown. Do keep in mind, however, that when all is said and done, it basically comes down to one person's opinion—mine in this case—and the prices listed here are only meant to provide collectors or dealers with an approximate value of a particular item.

Factors Affecting Value

Potential buyers should carefully consider the following questions before purchasing. If a piece is not perfect, what is its condition? Is that condition acceptable? Will it be easy to resell in its present condition? Is it a common or rare piece? How much is the seller asking? And, most importantly, how badly do you want the piece?

Condition

Keep in mind that values shown are based on what I call "average price for average condition." Basing values on some standard such as "mint" condition does a real disservice to all collectors, mainly because most vintage pieces found today are not in mint, or even near-mint, condition. In fact, most pieces are found in excellent or "8" condition, or what I call "average" (see page 22 for Condition Guide). For that reason, prices shown in this book use the "8" condition as the standard. Pieces found in better condition will, of course, command higher prices, while those in lesser condition will be valued lower. This system is designed for flexibility, allowing both buyers and sellers to describe actual condition in an objective manner, whether positive or negative, in order to give each party a better bargaining position.

As more collectors become concerned about their collections, the demand for higher quality pieces continues. The result is that choice pieces in mint or near-mint condition continue to rise sharply, while pieces in average condition increase at a slower pace and, in many cases, items in poor condition do not increase in value at all.

The values shown here are not meant to be absolute. Rather, they are offered to you as a guide to assist you in making informed decisions. Remember, when a transaction is taking place, the buyer and seller ultimately determine the value.

Future Value of Coca-Cola Collectibles

Tracking the Coca-Cola collectibles market is like tracking the stock market. All of us have seen specific areas of the collectibles market rise and fall. Baseball cards, PEZ, toys, slot machines, etc. can be red-hot one year but cool off the next. Coca-Cola memorabilia, because of the wide range that is available, will also experience areas that are very hot for a period, followed by a period of little activity. But Coca-Cola memorabilia generally is, and has been, a good solid growth collectible. One must also understand that a slowdown in a particular area of collecting is both normal and expected, especially after a long period of growth. Some consider this a weakening in the market, when in fact it is just the market correcting itself.

The past and present are relatively easy to understand and explain, but what about the future? Will interest in this beautiful memorabilia remain strong? Will items continue to rise in value? Will new collectors continue to enter the market?

I, for one, remain very optimistic. I have watched this market grow from the early 1970s, when all the known collectors could have held a meeting in a phone booth, through the 1980s and 1990s, which saw steady growth and consistent numbers of new collectors entering the market. I have no reason to doubt that this market will continue on its present course because Coca-Cola is a superior product.

History of The Coca-Cola Company

The history of Coca-Cola is one of the most remarkable stories in American business. The creator of the drink, Dr. John Stith Pemberton, began his career as a pharmacist and became successful developing and selling proprietary medicines. Pemberton's desire to create the perfect medicine and drink led him to experimenting with a substance derived from coca leaves that was supposed to aid digestion and extend life.

In 1886, Pemberton also developed a coca and cola drink that according to legend, he tried out at the Venable soda fountain at Jacob's Pharmacy in Atlanta. To produce and promote the drink on a commercial scale, Pemberton and his partner, Ed Holland, started the Pemberton Chemical Company with two other businessmen, including Frank Robinson, who named the drink Coca-Cola. Pemberton received a patent for the drink in June 1887.

In early 1888, an Atlanta pharmacist named Asa Candler, who was searching for new products, became interested in Coca-Cola. Candler quickly bought interests owned by others, and after the death of Pemberton later that year, gained control of the company.

With the sales of Coca-Cola soaring, Candler sought to spread out his sales and shares in his new company, and he found an investor in Boston. Seth Fowle & Sons, Proprietary Druggists, bought 50 shares of stock along with all rights to the New England area for the next 20 years. It proved to be a great move. The New England area was flooded with advertising, and sales skyrocketed.

By 1895, the product Coca-Cola was being sold in every state and territory in the United States. As the 1890s were coming to an end, The Coca-Cola Company slowly reduced its medicinal claims, and many ads and advertising pieces simply claimed that Coca-Cola was "Delicious and Refreshing." This practice continued as Congress passed a tax on proprietary medicines, and not beverages. With the Internal Revenue Service ruling that Coca-Cola was a drug, it was ordered to pay the tax. A long battle with the government continued until it was finally decided in 1902 that Coca-Cola was indeed a soft drink. However, as the turn of the century came to an end, occasional mention of "Relief for Headache" and other benefits remained.

During the last half of the 1890s, syrup plants and branch offices were opened in Dallas, Chicago, Los Angeles, Philadelphia, and New York City to meet growing demand. Just before the turn of the century, in July of 1899, an event took place that changed the course of the company's history. Two lawyers from Tennessee, Benjamin Franklin Thomas and Joseph Brown Whitehead, contracted with Asa Candler to sell Coca-Cola in bottles. This was the beginning of a franchising system that set the stage for the company to grow to the colossal business that it is today.

Their timing was perfect because by 1900, the cumbersome, difficult-to-use Hutchinson stoppered bottles were being replaced with a bottle whose lip allowed a metal crown to be crimped and sealed over it. The crown changed the course of the bottling industry and the impact on collectors of these early bottling attempts is tremendous. Hutchinson bottles are becoming more valuable as collectors insist on having examples of them in their collections. Values of these bottles have increased steadily over the years.

Brown and Whitehead's enterprise was so successful that by the following decade 379 bottling plants were operating. Although the product was the same, the bottles varied from bottler to bottler. The lack of uniformity soon ended, however.

The Coca-Cola Company was positioning itself for a period of growth that was unprecedented, but first it had to correct some problems. From the beginning, as Coca-Cola gained popularity, the company battled off hoards of imitators who attempted to capitalize on this product's success. While Harold Hirsh was in full charge of The Coca-Cola Company's legal affairs and continually fought and won these battles with the imitators in the courts, he became increasingly frustrated with the lack of uniformity in Coca-Cola bottles.

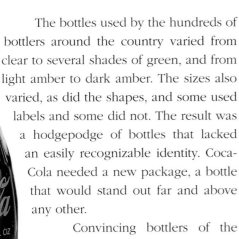

The bottles used by the hundreds of bottlers around the country varied from clear to several shades of green, and from light amber to dark amber. The sizes also varied, as did the shapes, and some used labels and some did not. The result was a hodgepodge of bottles that lacked an easily recognizable identity. Coca-Cola needed a new package, a bottle that would stand out far and above any other.

Convincing bottlers of the need for an expensive new bottle wasn't easy, but at the 1914 Bottlers Convention, Hirsch stressed the importance of investing then for the protection it would bring later. In June of 1915, a number of glass manufacturers were asked to create a distinctive package for Coca-Cola.

It was an employee of The Root Glass Company who came up with an unusual sample that would later become known as the "Hobbleskirt" design. The design was accepted at the Coca-Cola Bottlers Convention in 1916. Getting all the bottlers to switch over to the more expensive bottle would take a number of years, however.

Along with the bottling sales successes went continued success with syrup sales through soda fountains. The sale of syrup in 1900 was 370,877 gallons and increased to one million gallons annually by 1904. The combination of popular soda fountains and a progressive bottling industry marked a time of exceptional growth. By 1917, sales increased to over 12 million gallons annually. While serving as mayor of Atlanta, Asa G. Candler decided to give his business to his wife and five children, keeping only seven shares in his name. Less than two years later, on September 12, 1919, they sold the company to Ernest Woodruff, backed by The Trust Company of Georgia, of which Woodruff was President. Ernest Woodruff expanded the facilities of The Coca-Cola Company and added a syrup plant in New Orleans in 1919.

The advertising created by The Coca-Cola Company during the teens was fabulous. The company had a vision of what the "all American girl" looked like, and demanded it on its advertising. The girls, even though different models, had the same look—the eyes, parted mouth, and hair—that idealized the "girl next door" look. These models featured on calendars are the highlight of collectible Coca-Cola advertising during the teens.

By 1923, Robert Winship Woodruff, the 33-year-old son of Ernest Woodruff, took over as president of The Coca-Cola Company. The Woodruff era was to mark a dramatic change in the advertising of Coca-Cola. The D'arcy Advertising Company took on the Coca-Cola account at the same time Robert Woodruff took over presidency of The Coca-Cola Company, mainly because D'arcy employee Archie Laney Lee, a former reporter for the *Atlanta Georgian*, was a personal friend of Woodruff. The business relationship strengthened their personal relationship, and the results had an incredible positive effect on the company's advertising that would last for the next quarter of a century.

With the adoption of the Hobbleskirt bottle in 1916, Robert Woodruff felt it necessary to continue the process of standardization. The next big move to create uniformity among the bottlers came in 1924, with the formation of a standardization committee. Woodruff felt that Coca-Cola in bottles was the future of The Coca-Cola Company.

The committee, headed by Charles V. Rainwater, held its first meeting and recommended a standard design for trucks, cases, stationery, checks, and many other things, including uniforms for drivers. Subsequent meetings resulted in the development of standardized plans for bottling plants.

With standardization in place and in light of Woodruff's favorable feelings toward bottle sales, he called for increased advertising that emphasized Coca-Cola in bottles. The policy showed big results from 1923 to 1928. While fountain sales grew 20 percent, bottle sales increased by 65 percent.

By 1925 The Coca-Cola Company was advertising its product nationwide on billboards, and in 1927, it began using commercial radio. Many other groundbreaking advertising campaigns went into effect in the 1920s. Archie Lee's use of the word "Pause" in Coca-Cola advertising led

to one of the greatest expressions of American advertising: "The Pause That Refreshes."

The late 1920s also saw the first "big city" electric sign, spectacular in New York's Times Square. During the Depression of the early and mid-1930s, Lee continued creating advertising landmarks by hiring artist Haddon Sundblom, who annually produced the now iconic images of Santa Claus drinking Coca-Cola.

During the early 1930s, The Coca-Cola Company began associating Coca-Cola with food. The slogan "Natural Partner of Good Things to Eat" continued the process of showing that Coca-Cola is more than just a drink for when you are thirsty. Good at home, at work, with food and everywhere!

In the 1930s, the calendar girls were replaced by the "down home" images of young boys fishing, with great art-

work by Norman Rockwell, N.C. Wyeth, and others. Since calendars were mainly brought into the home, these images were important to The Coca-Cola Company, which wished to portray Coca-Cola as a family drink that was as popular with children as with adults. The connection of Coca-Cola at home carried through the late 1930s with the introduction of the open-top six-bottle carton, letting consumers know that it was "So easy to take home."

Archie Lee continued to develop groundbreaking advertising, including the use of the trademark "Coke" making its first appearance in national advertising in 1941. In 1942 "Coke" was highlighted by the image of "The Little Sprite," or what collectors now call "The Sprite Boy." This little pixie, created by Archie Lee and delineated by Haddon Sundblom, helped emphasize the connection between "Coke" and "Coca-Cola."

As America entered World War II, Robert Woodruff set the direction of The Coca-Cola Company's business efforts by stating "We will see that every man in uniform gets a bottle of Coca-Cola for five cents wherever he is and whatever it costs." During the war, 64 bottling operations were set up as close to battle areas as possible, and more than 5 billion bottles of Coke were consumed by the armed forces.

Wartime advertising produced by The Coca-Cola Company is always of special interest to collectors. Because of the war effort, metal was not used in advertising, which meant no serving trays, tin signs, etc. With wood and masonite replacing the tin signs, companies that produced specialty advertising like Kay Displays, Inc., flourished. Magazine advertising was increased with beautiful,

colorful patriotic ads showing our servicemen and women in uniform. These gave the country a sense of pride. The war effort showed up in much of the company's advertising with sets of signs called "Airplane Hangers" depicting our aircraft winning the air battles of the war. This wartime advertising is always very popular among collectors, with the cream of the crop being a set of cardboard cutouts showing servicewomen from the five branches of the military enjoying a glass or bottle of Coke. Produced in a small set as well as a full-size set, these are certainly among the best advertising done during this period.

With the war over and our servicemen returning, the United States was preparing for a period of prosperity and relaxation. The 1950s saw the servicemen home with their families, picnics, ballgames and leisure time—meaning Coke time—and Americans drank it like never before. It took The Coca-Cola Company until 1944 to sell its first billion gallons of syrup, with the second billion gallons being sold by 1953. With the leisure and fun times of the early '50s came an influx of picnic coolers by The Coca-Cola Company. The need to keep Coke cold at ballgames, picnics and the beach was important, so picnic coolers became very popular. Because of this, most of the picnic coolers from the '50s and '60s are fairly common today.

The 1950s added a whole new dimension to Coca-Cola advertising—television. The Coca-Cola Company sponsored a Thanksgiving special in 1950 that featured Edgar Bergen and Charlie McCarthy marking their first TV appearance. This show was followed by the Christmas special *One Hour in Wonderland*, starring Edgar Bergen and Walt Disney's animated characters.

In the later '50s, Coca-Cola and Disney teamed up again, sponsoring *The Mickey Mouse Club*. Because of the baby boom of post-World War II, The Coca-Cola Company felt it important to reach children, and what better way than via television. In 1951 it sponsored *The Adventures of Kit Carson*, starring Bill Williams. The popular cowboy was a big hit with the kids. In 1953, seeking to appeal to all age groups, they sponsored Eddie Fisher in *Coke Time*, another popular show that resulted in exactly what Coca-Cola was looking for: a family show with appeal beyond just the kids. These early television shows resulted in a tremendous amount of related material to collect, from records, toys, premiums, posters and magazine ads to a cardboard cutout of Eddie Fisher. These TV-related collectibles are very popular with a generation that remembers these shows so vividly.

In 1954, a chain of hamburger stands owned by two brothers named McDonald were bought out by Ray Kroc. With his hamburgers and fries he offered customers Coca-Cola, starting a relationship that proved to be fantastic for both McDonald's and Coca-Cola.

By 1962, J. Paul Austin became the president of The Coca-Cola Company. Austin, a graduate of Harvard Law School who commanded a PT Boat in World War II, would lead The Coca-Cola Company into a whole new decade with the addition the newly created diet drink, Tab. In 1963, Coca-Cola needed a song—a theme that would sum up Coca-Cola in one short verse—and found it in "Things Go Better With Coke." The 1963 "Things Go Better" campaign created a whole new area of collectibles, including music boxes, musical lighters, novelties, signs, and a whole new "fresh" look to Coca-Cola advertising.

These 1960s collectibles are becoming more and more popular. By 1965 the soft drink industry was doing very well, with an annual 260 drinks per capita, and Coca-Cola holding 41 percent of the market. The mid-1960s also saw the addition of Minute Maid Orange Juice and Hi-C to The Coca-Cola family. These new products were advertised as refreshing drinks that could be enjoyed any time of the day.

By the late 1960s, a new Coke theme song was developed. The song "It's the Real Thing" flooded the airwaves. At the same time, The Coca-Cola Company felt it needed a new look and hired the New York firm of Lippincott and Margulies to create it. The result was the "Dynamic Ribbon" or as collectors call it, the "Wave Logo," which brings us to the end of the era of the classic collectibles that this book encompasses.

Coca-Cola Art

Certainly one of the main reasons why collectors are drawn to the advertising of The Coca-Cola Company is the beautiful artwork produced by some of the country's top artists working for the best advertising agencies. For the most part, these artists remain unnamed, sort of the "unsung" heroes of Coca-Cola collectors. Of course the big names that we are all familiar with like Rockwell, Sundblom, Wyeth, and Stanley have become part of the vocabulary of collectors. Most of the other artists who produced this beautiful art are unfamiliar to the majority of the collecting community.

This art was not produced by The Coca-Cola Company in Atlanta, but rather by advertising agencies from around the country who produced the art, hired models, put complete campaigns together, contracted with printing companies for production, and in many cases, actually shipped advertising material to local bottlers.

Account executives from an advertising company like Snyder & Black, which produced for many years the quality pieces that we all search for, traveled to Atlanta to meet with the advertising department. These meetings resulted in ideas from both sides, outlining the campaign or needs for the following year's advertising. With outline in hand, the agency directed artists as to what was needed. Copywriters filled in the blank spaces and create slogans, newspaper, and magazine ad copy, billboards—whatever needed words. In some cases the advertising for a campaign revolved around a particular piece of art or a slogan. The image of the Sprite Boy or the slogan "Refresh Yourself" is a perfect example. Developing the art was a process beginning with rough or conceptual art. In this first step, art was often rejected or changed to meet the requirements of the particular campaign.

With rough art and strategy complete, artists then created composition art or "comps." These were basically refined pieces of rough art, usually pencil drawings and watercolor. This composition art, along with copy, slogans, and campaign strategy, was then taken back to Atlanta for another meeting. Approvals, rejections and changes to numerous pieces of art and copy resulted in a fine tuning of the campaign. The approved comps were then returned to the artists for the creation of original art. In many cases, artists were chosen for their particular specialty. The importance of the distinctive bottle and how it appeared on the final piece of art was of the utmost importance. Often the bottle or six-pack carton was added afterwards by another artist who specialized in this area of art.

Over the years, The Coca-Cola Company became interested in particular artists and requested their work. Many were the obvious names previously mentioned—favorites like Norman Rockwell, N.C. Wyeth, Fred Mizen, Fredric Stanley, and others who were in demand to produce artwork that The Coca-Cola Company felt best captured the image or look that they wanted to present to the buying public.

One of these artists, probably the best known to all Coca-Cola collectors, was Haddon Sundblom. His art,

whether it be man, woman, or child, or the legendary image of Santa Claus, was the epitome of what The Coca-Cola Company felt their product stood for—the wholesome all-American, just-plain-folks look that made people feel good.

How is artwork of particular artists identified? Well, it's not easy. Most of this art was not signed, or the signature does not appear on the finished (printed) piece. The reason for this is simple. While advertising art provided a reliable source of income, most artists didn't like working on a schedule or painting an image that was required and not "created." Pre-defined work, deadlines, and constant changes did not fit well with their lifestyle.

Signing a piece of art was not that important to them, or in many cases just did not fit in with the image, and it was removed during the printing process. While a signature by a well-known artist like Norman Rockwell usually was not removed, even art that he produced for Coca-Cola can be found unsigned.

Original artwork, including sketches, comps, rough art and original oil paintings are among the most desirable and prestigious of all Coca-Cola memorabilia—as well as being the most valuable—with paintings by Rockwell, Sundblom, Wyeth and others going for hundreds of thousands of dollars. But those are the exceptions, not the rule. Quality original art has changed hands for hundreds of dollars and in the thousands for original paintings.

The value of original art is based on the individual piece, but general guidelines apply. The most valuable piece is an original oil painting of a "recognizable" image, signed by a well-known artist. Less value is given if the artist is unknown. A "recognizable" piece of art is an image that was actually used as an advertising piece, and can be identified, like a cardboard sign or calendar. Next would be a recognizable piece of art that remains unsigned (the difference between signed and unsigned art could be thousands of dollars.) And, finally, a piece that is not recognizable and is unsigned would certainly be desirable, but not in the high dollar range. Sketches or rough art and comps are much more common, but are still prized pieces in any collection. For the most part, however, original art, and in particular an original painting, remains only a "dream piece" for even the most advanced Coca-Cola collector.

Collector Tips

General and Specialized Collecting

People enjoy collecting Coca-Cola memorabilia for many reasons. Surely one of the greatest attractions is the wide range of collectibles available. While most collectors collect anything with the famous Coca-Cola logo, others are specialized collectors.

Because of the expense involved, it may be difficult for one collector to amass a great collection encompassing all areas. But that same collector could have a fantastic collection in one specific area. Many enjoy collecting only Coca-Cola bottles, for example. Others have set a goal to own every tray or calendar the company has produced. But when trying to track down items from the early or pre-1900s, they suddenly realize that it is quite a task.

One of my favorite specialized areas of collecting, and one that even the new collector can get into without spending a fortune, is postcards. Any postcard showing a nice Coca-Cola sign is a good item. Postcards are easy to find, and early ones are very desirable. But whether you collect everything or choose to specialize, you'll always have a good feeling when you add an attractive piece to your collection.

Evaluating Condition

Condition is the most important factor in determining the value of an item. That's why it's so difficult to put a value on an item in a book like this. People often don't consider condition. This is a major error. The price should always reflect the piece's condition.

It would be a mistake to purchase a piece for $50 because it is in the price guide for $50 but the condition is poor. You should point out to the dealer any flaws in the piece, and the price should be adjusted accordingly.

I have always been in favor of the "upgrade" system of collecting. This means buying a piece that's available now, but buying a better piece when it becomes available and selling the lesser piece to help pay for the better one. Keep in mind that it's not easy to resell pieces in poor condition, so be sure to consider condition carefully when purchasing.

Detecting Fakes and Reproductions

It's unfortunate but true: fakes and reproductions are a part of collecting. Whether it be Coca-Cola items, Ming vases or teddy bears, reproductions are everywhere. The trick is to keep your mistakes to a minimum, and the best way to do that is plain and simple education. Read everything available and ask questions. Put your mistakes behind you and learn from them. Also, tell other collectors about items that you know are phony.

Finding out if a piece is original or reproduction is important, but questioning the dealer is not always the answer. Don't be fooled by appearance. Many pieces can be instantly aged by unscrupulous dealers who are looking to make a buck from a collector anxious to make a major find.

I wish there were a perfect way to distinguish a reproduction from an original, but there isn't. I suggest seeing the original, holding it in your hands and feeling it. In many cases, this is the best and surest method of not getting burnt.

Tall Tales: Discerning Truth from Fiction

People who deal in antiques and collectibles sometimes attempt to enhance a piece with a fictitious or embellished history to add to its mystique. The challenge is to separate fact from fiction, and learning about what you collect is the best way to do this.

The people who make up these stories usually don't have the correct information to back up the fantasy they have created. It's your job as a collector to get as much information as you can and then analyze it to determine the truth. You probably have already heard some of the stories: found in a warehouse, bought from an old bottling plant, discovered in the rafters of an old house or in an old woman's trunk that has never been opened, and my personal favorite: acquired from an old store that has been boarded up since 1920.

Unfortunately, most of these old stories are used to enhance a phony piece rather than an original piece. Rely on common sense rather than the story to make the decision whether to buy or not. Many people have told me "the piece can't be a phony because the dealer told me he bought it from a woman who had it for fifty years." Do your homework, study the trademark logos on pieces used over the years and how they have changed. So, if a piece is presented to you as found in a treasure chest that has been buried since 1905, but the trademark logo is of 1950s vintage, you'll know right away the piece is phony. (See Coca-Cola Script Trademarks on page 23.)

One of my pet peeves is the misuse of words or phrases like "rare," "very rare," "only one known to

exist," "never seen before," "the only one I have ever seen," "one of only three known"—the list goes on, but you get the idea. Take these stories and overused phrases with a grain of salt and realize that they are part of dealing in antiques and collectibles.

Cleaning and Restoring

Of all the tips one can give to the collector, this is certainly the most delicate. Can you imagine someone telling you how to clean and polish a tray, then trying it, only to find that you have totally destroyed it? Well, believe me, it's happened to people many times—especially with trays and metal signs.

Other than simple dusting, leave the piece alone unless you know exactly what you're doing. Some collectors have been successful with dirt removal, cleaning and polishing, but many have learned through trial and error. This is another area where education is important.

Touching up trays or signs is also difficult. It should never be done without complete knowledge of what you're doing. Keep in mind that a tray that's been touched up, whether or not it is a good job, does not have the same value as a piece that hasn't been touched up. Many times a touched-up piece is difficult to sell.

The same rules apply to paper collectibles. Don't do anything unless you know what you are doing. I do strongly recommend protecting paper items, especially calendars, in an album or frame. And finally, always choose a frame shop that uses acid-free mat board and is knowledgeable about paper preservation.

Buying Restored Pieces

When buying a piece for resale or for your collection, it's important to know if it has been restored. Ask the seller what has been done, examine the piece carefully, looking for breaks in the paper or uneven color. If the piece is framed, ask if you may take it out to examine it, as framing and matting can hide damage. If the dealer won't let you take it out, be very skeptical. Also be sure when buying a piece that it can be returned if you discover it has been restored after being told it wasn't. From a collector's standpoint, you would like everything in your collection to be in original mint condition, but this isn't realistic, especially with something as delicate and rare as early paper. You should be aware that a piece of restored advertising, no matter how rare or how well that restoration was done, can't be called mint and will never have the value of a unrestored piece, even if looks unrestored.

You must decide if restored pieces are acceptable, and if so, how limited or extensive the restoration can be. There will always be a range of standards for restoration among collectors, and setting standards for your collection is your choice, not mine or any other collector's. However, when setting your standard, keep in mind the potential appreciation and resale value of your pieces.

Collecting Coca-Cola as an Investment

Many collectors of Coca-Cola memorabilia consider themselves only collectors and not investors. This is a mistake. People collect for different reasons—they enjoy the hunt, they are taken by the visual appeal or perhaps they like owning of a piece of the history of The Coca-Cola Company. But regardless of your motivation for collecting, every dime spent on a collection is money that had to be earned, and that makes your collection an investment.

The same rules apply with buying collectibles as with any other investment. Most important is to know the market in which you are dealing, getting as much information about Coca-Cola collectibles as possible. People who invest in the stock market research the market and the company they are seeking to invest in. The same thing has to be done when buying a piece for a collection. To determine if a piece is a good investment, use the following guidelines.

The first is a very touchy one and I'm sure to get flack over it, but I suppose I'm just a Coca-Cola purist. I really believe that buying newer items is not a good investment. I have been buying and selling Coca-Cola pieces for a long time, and prices for vintage pieces have risen year after year, but not for the reproduction, fantasy and newer collectible items.

Many think the size of a collection is very important. I've heard many boast of having thousands of pieces in their collection, and to accomplish this they will buy anything and everything bearing the Coca-Cola logo. Don't fall into this trap! Many of the recently produced items for the collectibles market that sell for $5 to $10 today may not even be worth what you paid for them 10 to 15 years from now. If you ask anyone who has tried to sell a collection loaded with commemorative and newer items, you'll find that it's not easy. Even when the collection is sold, the collector usually ends up taking a loss.

On the other hand, those who have sold collections of original advertising pieces found it easy and have made large profits. I would rather have a smaller collection of quality older items than a larger collection of newer items. When I say "older," I don't necessarily mean items from the '30s rather than the '50s, but rather items that weren't purposely produced for today's collectible market. Because these "made for the collector's market" items are made in huge quantities, they won't appreciate in value and don't make good investments.

However, "made for the collector's market" items do serve at least one purpose. They introduce new collectors to the hobby, and a percentage of them trickle down to collecting vintage items. This continual influx is what keeps me so positive about the future. And there's nothing wrong with buying "made for the collector's market" items, as long as you're buying them for enjoyment and not for an investment.

Financing Your Collection

Over the past 20 years, I've seen the prices of Coca-Cola collectibles rise constantly, and unless you have just hit the lottery or are independently wealthy, it can be very difficult to amass a nice collection. But there are ways to finance your collection as long as you are willing to spend some money.

I have heard many people say that they have passed up a worthwhile piece because they already have it in their collection. This is a mistake. If you are at a show and see an item that you feel is priced right, you should buy it, even if you have it or if it is in a different area than your collection. You can sell it for a profit or use it for trade.

Another good way to make money is to create a list of items for sale, such as upgrade items or duplicates. Advertise in a club newsletter. Let other collectors know that you have a list of items for sale. (Remember to keep close

track of what you pay for items and what you sell them for.) Soon you will have a little nest egg for use when you want to purchase a special piece for your collection.

Finding Coca-Cola Collectibles

When people see my collection, one of the first things they ask is: "Where do you find all this stuff?" It isn't easy, and it takes a lot of time and hard work to build a collection. Even if you have a fortune to spend, it isn't always that easy to find quality pieces. For this reason alone, Coca-Cola collecting is a challenge, and adding a beautiful piece to a collection becomes exciting.

It's important to let collectors know who and where you are and what your interest is. One must also keep abreast of what is happening in the field of antiques and collectibles. Subscribing to publications such as *Antique Trader* and other newspapers and magazines devoted to collectors is one of the most important links to people who have pieces for sale, and an excellent way to let people know your wants. These publications also list antique shows and auctions in and out of your area. I have a good friend who travels often, and he never leaves home with-

Getting Involved in the Collector Community

Becoming involved in the collecting community is important. Know who the collectors are and where their interests lie. Most Coca-Cola pieces change hands between existing collectors, either through the upgrade system or through collectors selling off individual pieces or sections of their collections. Read books and, of course, ask questions. Find out what pieces were recently found and for how much they sold. Know the market and remember that an informed and knowledgeable collector is a collector who will eventually end up with a good collection. I can't tell you how many times I have heard comments like, "I've been collecting for years, and thought I was the only one!" and "I had no idea this stuff was worth this much!" The more you know about the subject, the better off you'll be.

Try to meet and get to know collectors with interests similar to yours. Asking them questions, and possibly seeing their collections, is very helpful in making informed decisions regarding your own collection. Don't be afraid to let people know what you collect.

I find that networking with other collectors is the best way to stay abreast of this ever-changing market. Call or e-mail fellow collectors to find out what you may have missed. I have also found that networking helps the market eliminate phony collectibles.

Buying Through Internet Auctions

Large numbers of Coca-Cola items are now sold on Internet auction sites such as eBay. While these sites provide a convenient and popular way to buy and sell, they can involve more risk than buying or selling in person. Sellers typically include photos as well as descriptions, but photos don't show every flaw, and descriptions can be inaccurate.

One safeguard is the feedback system, in which buyers and sellers rate each other on their satisfaction. If you choose to use an Internet auction site, make sure you

out checking the *Antique Trader* to see what shows will be taking place in the area where he will be traveling.

Check auction listings in antique and other publications as well. Many good Coke pieces have been hidden away in a general auction with no competition from other collectors. Subscribe to auctions and try to get on mailing lists of auction houses, even if they don't specialize in Coke or advertising items. Coca-Cola pieces turn up in most auctions eventually.

Stay alert. Don't assume that an all-furniture auction, for example, has no Coke items in it. Ask questions to be sure. Large antique shows all over the country sell anything and everything in antiques and collectibles, while many other shows specialize in advertising, coin-op, paper items, toys, etc. All of these are good sources of Coca-Cola memorabilia. Know when and where they are, and then be there.

Some collectors find placing inexpensive "want ads" in local papers to be a great source of items right in their own backyard. Local antique shops are another important stop. Go to the ones in your area on a regular basis, leave your card, let them know your interests, and ask them to give you a call if anything turns up.

Many towns have areas heavy with antique shops or malls that specialize in antiques and collectibles. Year-round, weekend antique shows are also very popular. Find out where they are and visit them, perhaps as part of a day trip or a long weekend with the family. Buying nice stuff and building a good collection takes work. Coca-Cola pieces don't come to you—you have to go out and find them.

check the potential buyer's or seller's feedback. If you have questions, be sure to e-mail or call the person and get satisfactory answers before bidding. Also be sure you know the payment, shipping, insurance and return policies.

Buying at Live Auctions

Live auctions are great sources of Coca-Cola collectibles because they display excellent artwork. Many pieces were saved and turn up at house sales and auctions. Be sure to subscribe to mail auctions and antiques publications, and make sure you're aware of sales in and out of your area. Many auction houses will accept absentee bids, so don't be afraid to ask and to use your phone. It can save you a lot of wasted time. I can't tell you how many miles I have traveled to auctions because a creative auctioneer listed in his advertisement "very rare Coke tray" only to find a 1950 tray that looked like it had been run over by a truck.

On the other hand, though, I took a six-hour trip to an auction that listed a Coke sign that turned out to be one of the most important pieces I have ever purchased. Those pieces are the ones that make it all worthwhile.

Get to know your local auctioneers. If you trust them, tell them your interests. Believe me, the next time they have a Coke piece, they'll let you know. If a piece is listed in the advertisement, make a call and ask for a description and the condition. Go to the sale preview, but don't run up to the piece and reveal your enthusiasm.

Another tip, as difficult as it may be, is to set a limit on what you will spend. Many great Coke pieces have sold at auctions far below their value because they just didn't have the right audience. But many pieces have sold far above their value because the right group of people was in the room.

Keeping Records

It's extremely important to keep an accurate, up-to-date record of every piece in your collection. Remember, you're investing as well as collecting. Every piece that you spend money on or trade for is an investment that should be recorded. List every piece with its date of purchase or sale, amount paid, condition, and any other pertinent details.

If you have been collecting for some time and haven't done this, do so as quickly as possible. Listing each and every item is a big job, but believe me, it should be done. This is also important if you decide to sell your collection or perhaps leave it to a spouse or children. A current record is the backbone of every collection.

Insuring

Not being an insurance agent or knowing your collection, I can't tell you how to insure it. But I can give you some hints. You shouldn't assume that your collection is covered on your homeowner's policy. Don't assume anything when it comes to insurance. Call your agent, invite him to inspect your collection and get his advice. If you're not happy with what your agent tells you, call another and then another if necessary, until you find a policy that you feel comfortable with.

Collections can be insured in several ways; for example, you could increase your homeowner's policy by adding a rider that covers the collection. Or you could possibly take out a "fine arts" policy to cover some of the more expensive items.

You may be required to keep a photographic record of your collection for your insurance company. This, by the

way, is something that I recommend whether it is required or not. Try to set a minimum value for the items that are to be photographed.

Displaying

Proper framing is essential to protect your investment. Make sure the person doing the framing uses the proper paper conservation methods and is aware of the value and importance of the piece. It's extremely important that the framer doesn't do anything to the piece that you haven't discussed, like gluing, trimming or removing anything from it, such as a metal strip or calendar page. Also, make sure the framer is insured to cover your piece while it is in his possession, and put that on your receipt with the value. Point out the importance of using acid-free mats and backing as well as using a spacer such as a mat so the printed piece doesn't touch the glass. If the edges of the piece are sharp with no tears or edgewear, don't cover the edge with a mat, so if you should ever decide to sell it, the potential buyer can see that nothing is hidden.

Be sure pieces aren't exposed to high humidity or direct sunlight. Hooded frame lights work well for small quality pieces, but track lighting is best for large areas. The ability to move individual lights to eliminate glare is a big advantage, but eliminating all glare from a room with many framed pieces is just not possible. Using nonglare glass in frames can help, but I personally don't use it because it dulls the colors.

Serving trays and tin signs require a lot more attention and should be checked periodically when displayed. Some people do frame certain trays and tin signs, and that's fine, but make sure a sealed, framed piece can breathe, meaning it isn't airtight. Avoid areas with high humidity, and polish with a mild car wax once every year or two to prevent pitting. The best place to display tin is in an area with a fairly constant temperature.

Showcases are especially good for displaying pocket mirrors, watch fobs, knives and celluloid pieces. If you don't have room for a large showcase, small flat ones are available.

Storing

Paper signs, calendars and cardboard pieces that aren't displayed require proper care for storage. Purchase

sheets of foamcore and a roll of thin, clear acetate from an art supply store. Measure the piece and allow an extra quarter inch all around. Cut the foamcore to this size. Don't attach the piece to the foamcore with tape or glue; simply place the piece face-up on the foamcore, then flip the foamcore and sign face-down on a rolled-out section of acetate. Cut the acetate, leaving plenty of excess. Pull the acetate tightly across the back of the foamcore, and tape it. Cut the ends, and again pull tightly and tape. Foamcore and acetate aren't cheap, but the cost is well worth the protection.

To move or store trays, always put them in clear plastic bags. This is the best way to protect them from scratching.

Flat paper items like blotters, coupons, magazine ads, letterheads and other paper collectibles are best kept in plastic sleeves that can be filed in a three-ring binder for easy access. Books, paper items and other collectibles can be stored in corrugated file boxes. Pack the items, label the outside of the boxes and store them off the ground in a dry area.

Condition Guide

The condition of any Coca-Cola collectible is the most important factor in determining its value. Collectors use two types of grading systems. Nowadays, the "Poor" to "Mint" system seems to be used less than the "1" to "10" method. Shown below are both systems with representative photos of a 1934 tray. Please keep in mind when evaluating an item that it is not in anyone's interest to overgrade it.

10 — 9.5 — 9 	**Mint** New condition, unused, flawless, no visible marks or scratches. There is no middle ground in this category; it's either perfect or it's not. You can't say "It's Mint but it has a scratch." Mint = Perfect.
8.5	**Near Mint** Very minor or slight marks, chips, or scratches, a minor tear (on paper). Nothing serious that would detract from the color or beauty of the piece. This is the category most often misused.
8 — 7.5 	**Excellent +** Visible minor scratches, perhaps minor chips, minor tears or peeling of paper items. Excellent is the category most pieces fall into and the one that prices in this book are based on.
7 — 6.5 	**Excellent** Just a few more minor chips than normal, scratches, minor marks, but still not serious, a repairable tear on paper items. Still a very good looking piece and very collectible.
6 — 5.5 	**Very Good** This is the extreme low end of Excellent condition. Still collectible, but a few more problems; perhaps a white spot on a tray, slight pitting, edge chips and rubs, a few tears or a small piece out of the edge of paper items.
5 — 4.5 	**Good** Scratches, minor flaking, possibly minor dent and rust or pitting, serious tears, or portion missing on paper items. An OK item. This is the point when it becomes questionable whether the piece is collectible or not.
4 — 3.5 	**Fair** More than minor pitting and flaking, dents, trimmed or torn paper, fading or bad color. Collectible only if it's a rare piece; a good filler item.
3 — 2.5	**Poor** In worn state, with rust, dents, or pitting. A paper item that has been torn and repaired, possibly restored; generally not very collectible.
2 — 1.5 	**Poor** Extensive pitting and rust areas, extensive fading and wear, dents and bends, restoration work that has been done poorly. This would be an item that would not be collectible or have much value at all.
1 — 0	**Worthless** An item that has no redeemable qualities, something that you would not display regardless of rarity; something you didn't have to pay for.

The Coca-Cola Script Trademark

The story surrounding the creation of the Coca-Cola script trademark is an interesting one, and since it has never been disputed, the legend lives on. Pemberton's associate Frank Robinson named the product for two of its ingredients, changing the "K" in "Kola" to a "C." It was also Robinson, as the story goes, who penned the famous script lettering that is now so familar.

Following are many of the variations used over the years. Knowing them and when they were used can be helpful in determining age and detecting counterfeits. Keep in mind that many local Coca-Cola bottlers and companies producing advertising for Coca-Cola took liberties with the logos, in some cases altering or misusing them, or even using outdated logos, especially in the earlier years.

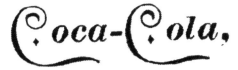

1880s-1892
Early script variation with diamonds

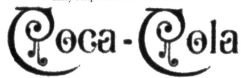

1890-1891
Unusual typestyle used on a number of calendars

1887-1890
Early script with line extending from first "O", and "Trade Mark" in tail; also no trademark in tail.

1893-1901
Crude script with "Trade-Mark" in tail, under tail or no trademark with "Trade Mark Registered" in tail 1901-1903

1898-1902
Custom script with "Trade-Mark" in tail; note open "O's", and unusual tails on "C's"

1903
Misused script "Trade-Mark Registered" in tail; used on some 1903 calendars.

1903-1931
Traditional script "Trade-Mark Registered" in tail

1930-1941
Traditional script "Trade-Mark Reg. U.S. Pat. Off." in tail

1941-1962
Traditional script "Reg. U.S. Pat. Off." under script

1950-Present
Traditional script "Trade Mark ®" under script

1958-1963
"Arciform" logo also called "Fishtail" logo by collectors

1970-Present
"Dynamic Ribbon" also called "Wave" logo; actually introduced in late 1969

Calendars

It isn't a coincidence that calendars appear first in this book. They have been, since my first day as a collector of Coca-Cola memorabilia, my main interest. I would have considered trading any tray or sign I owned for a particular calendar I needed.

Many people don't realize the importance of the calendar as a marketing tool in the days before radio or television. Of course, newspaper and magazine ads and signs brought the product before the public eye, but the calendar was much more than that. It was a useful product that was given away to consumers with the hope that they would hang them in their homes to remind them that Coca-Cola was "delicious and refreshing." It obviously worked, and worked well. The Coca-Cola Company realized this, producing at least one type of calendar every year beginning in 1891. In some cases, several calendars were produced in a year.

During my early years of collecting, only one group of price guides was available for Coca-Cola collectibles, and the discrepancies between the calendars shown in these guides and the calendars I was purchasing were obvious. It soon became clear that many of the calendar pads shown were switched or altered in some way. Those price guides, unfortunately, are still available, showing the misdated and altered calendars. With this book, I hope to clear up those discrepancies.

Prior to 1914, calendar sizes weren't very consistent. The size of a complete calendar (including pad) made between 1914 and 1919 is approximately 13" x 32". From 1920 to 1922, they measured 12" x 32". All of these calendars were equipped with a metal strip and hanger at the top.

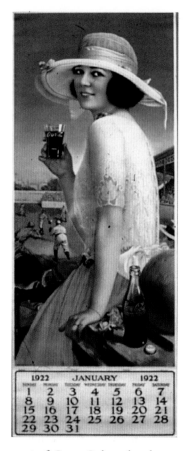

From 1923 to 1940, the size was approximately 12" x 24", again with metal strip and hanger. In 1926, however, the calendar changed drastically, measuring 10½" x 18⅝" and printed on medium-weight cardstock. It also had a hole drilled at the top for hanging (replacing the standard metal strip). This was also the first year that the calendar had a cover sheet over the pad. It simply said, "1926 Compliments of The Coca-Cola Co., Atlanta, GA." Cover sheets over the pad weren't standard until after 1930.

Another interesting aspect of Coca-Cola calendars is the glass and bottle variations. Because of the obvious difference between fountain and bottle sales, two calendars were issued in certain years, with one model holding a glass and the other a bottle. In some cases, one type of calendar may be rarer than the other, depending on how many have turned up over the years.

The following is a list of years in which calendars were printed with both glass and bottle versions: 1904, 1914, 1915, 1916, 1917, 1919 (knitting girl), 1920, 1923 and 1927. The 1923 bottle version is very unusual in that the bottle is embossed "8 oz." rather than the standard "6½ oz.," which was the size of the bottle used at that time.

The 1927 calendar also has a slightly different variation. On one calendar, a large bottle is inset with a border around it on the lower left-hand side, and another has no bottle at all.

The 1928 distributor calendar also has a glass variation. In 1918, and from 1921 to 1930 (with the exception of 1923 and 1927), calendars show both glass and bottle. From 1931 on, they show bottles only.

As any collector who actively seeks Coca-Cola calendars knows, they aren't easy to find. Any calendar before 1914 is considered rare, and any before 1910 is very rare. Despite the rarity of these early calendars, the value drops drastically if they are found without a pad or a sheet attached, or if they are trimmed from their original size.

After 1940, there was a major change in Coca-Cola calendars. From 1941 through the 1960s, they were made as multiple-page calendars, usually of six pages plus a cover sheet, with two months on each page.

The condition of the calendar, as with any Coca-Cola collectible, is most important in determining value. The prices you see on calendars in this book reflect examples in clean, presentable condition. Examples in poor condition or without a pad will certainly be worth less, and mint untouched examples could certainly be worth more.

Keep the following things in mind when purchasing a calendar. First, be sure that it has not been trimmed from its original size. (The measurement information provided earlier should be helpful.)

The pad or sheet attached is also important. Make sure it is the correct year for the calendar. If it is not a full pad, take note as to how many sheets are attached. One sheet attached (other than the last sheet) is acceptable as long as you realize that you are buying an altered calendar. If a calendar is trimmed or has a partial pad or no pad at all, or has been mounted to poster board, it can't be called mint.

Whether you are a die-hard calendar collector like me, or you just happen to have a few in your collection, I hope you'll agree that calendars are certainly the most beautiful of all Coca-Cola collectibles.

Condition plays a crucial role in value! Items in this book are priced based on a condition rating of "excellent" or "8" (see page 22 for Condition Guide). Items in mint condition, or "10," could be worth more than the listed price, while items in fair or poor condition could be worth much less. Every flaw must be taken into consideration. Even rare examples in poor condition will have much less value than those shown in this book.

The items shown in this chapter are just a cross-section of the vast amount of memorabilia that Coca-Cola has produced. This sampling, however, should give you a good idea of what is available and their general values.

Exact size and dates have been indicated where possible. Many, however, are estimates.

— Early Calendars —

Photo courtesy of Gordon Breslow

Photo courtesy of Gordon Breslow

1891, 6½" x 9" **$18,000**

1891, 6½" x 9" **$18,000**

Photo courtesy of Gordon Breslow

1896, 6½" x 9" **$25,000**

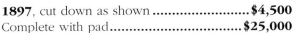

1897, cut down as shown **$4,500**
Complete with pad................................**$25,000**

1898, 7¼" x 12¾" **$20,000**

1899, 7⅜" x 13" **$15,000**

Photo courtesy of The Coca-Cola Co.

1900, 7¼" x 12¾" **$20,000**

1900, 7¼" x 12¾" **$20,000**

1901, 7⅝" x 11"..**$13,000**

1901, 7⅜" x 13"..**$8,500**

1902, 7½" x 14½"..**$10,000**

1903, 7¾" x 15"..**$7,000**
There are two versions of this calendar.

1904, 7¾" x 15"................................$6,500

1905, 7¾" x 15¼"................................$7,000

1906, 7" x 14¼"................................$8,000

1907, 7" x 14"................................$8,500

1908, 7" x 14" $7,000

1909, 11" x 20½" $10,000

1910, 8¾" x 17½" $7,500

1910, 15" x 26", "Happy Days" $13,000

1911, 10½" x 17¾" ....**$6,500**   **1912**, 9¾" x 19¾", small version **$6,000**

1913, 13½" x 22½" ....**$5,000**   **1913**, 16" x 28", bottler's calendar **$10,000**

1914...**$2,500**
With bottle (not shown)..............................**$6,500**

1915...**$6,500**
With bottle (not shown)..............................**$9,000**

1916, with bottle **$3,500**
With glass (not shown).................................**$3,500**

1917, with bottle **$4,500**

1918..**$9,500**

1919, with glass **$6,500**

1919, with bottle **$6,500**

1920, with glass **$4,000**

1922...$3,600

1923, with bottle $1,200

1924...$2,000

1925...$1,500

1926...$1,900

1927, glass only $1,800
With bottle inset (not shown).....................$1,600

1928 ....$2,000

1929..$2,000

1930 MARCH 1930

Sunday	Monday	Tuesday	Wednesday	Thursday	Friday	Saturday
		It Had to Be Good to Get Where It Is				1
2	3	4	5	6	7	8
9	10	11	12	13	14	15
16	17	18	19	20	21	22
23/30	24/31	25	26	27	28	29

1930.. $2,000

CARRY ME BACK TO OLD VIRGINNY

1934..**$1,000**

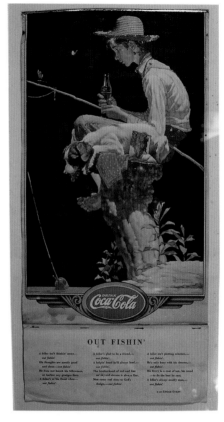

OUT FISHIN'

1935..**$850**

THROUGH ALL THE YEARS SINCE 1886

1886 **Coca-Cola** 1936

FIFTIETH ANNIVERSARY

1936..**$1,100**

IT'S THE REFRESHING THING TO DO

1937..**$850**

1938..**$850**

1940..**$850**

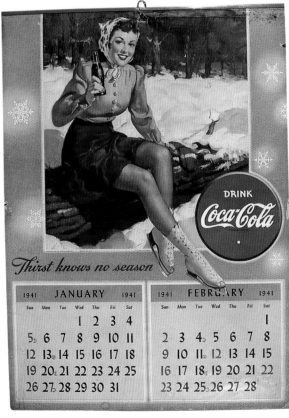

1941..**$550**

1942..**$450**

1944...$450

1945...$450

1946...$850

1948...$400

1949...$375

1951...$225

1950...$375

1952...$200

1953..$225

1954..$185

1955..$125

1956..$100

1957..$125

1958..$85

1959..$100

1960..$75

1961..$75

1962..$75

1963..$75

1964..$75

1965..**$75**

1966..**$75**

1967..**$75**

1968..**$75**

1969..**$75**

1970..**$75**

Distributor Calendars

1916, 8" x 15", Miss Pearl White
......................................**$5,000**
This calendar was a magazine insert piece.

1918, 5" x 9", June Caprice
.... **$500**

1919, 6¼" x 10½", Marion Davies
.... **$5,000**

1927, 7" x 13" **$2,000**

1928, 8" x 14" **$850**
This calendar was produced in other variations.

Bottlers' Calendars

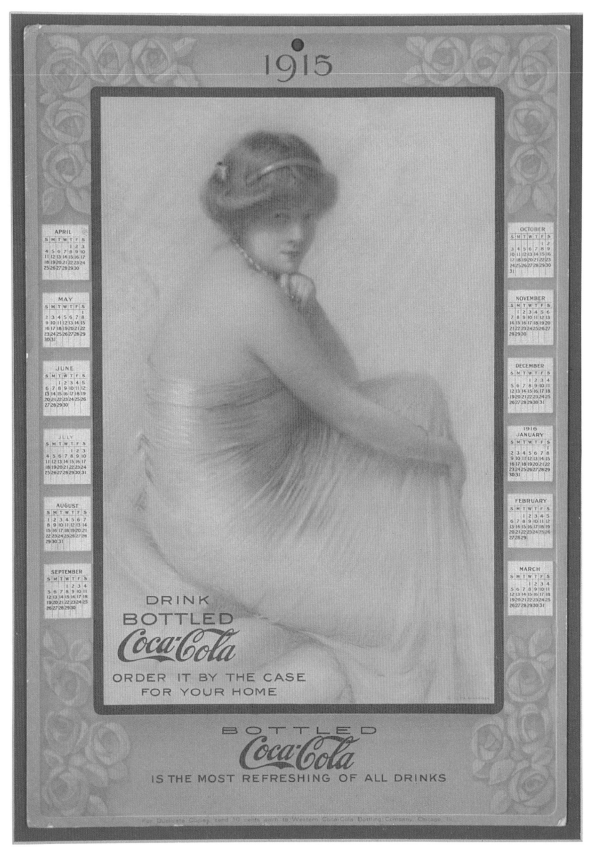

1915, Western Coca-Cola Bottlers **$6,500**

1928, Romney, W.V. **$3,500**

Photo courtesy of Gordon Breslow

1953, 16" x 33½", Kentucky Derby
.... **$1,800**

1946, 6½" x 11½", Art, Boy Scouts, Rockwell............................ **$400**

1949, 8" x 14½", Art, Boy Scouts, Rockwell........................... **$400**

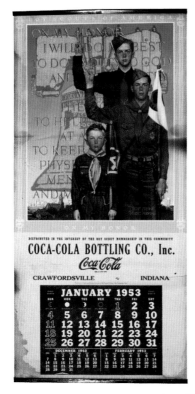

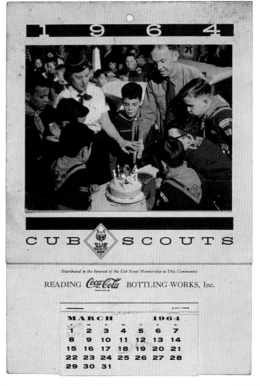

1958, 11" x 23", Art, Boy Scouts, Rockwell **$450**

1964, 7¼" x 10¼", Cub Scouts **$200**

1954...$20

1955...$20

1956...$20

1957...$18

1958...$18

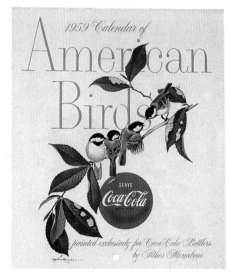

1959...$16

1961.......................... $12

1963... $12

1964... $12

1965.................................... $12

1966.................................... $12

1967.................................... $12

1968.................................... $10

When I first started collecting Coca-Cola memorabilia, serving trays were the main point of interest. It seemed that everyone's collection was judged by which trays they had and which trays they needed. Early price guides reflect this fact. While other items were shown, the most important were the serving trays. Even The Coca-Cola Company produced a book in 1970 called the *Catalog of Metal Service Trays and Art Plates Since 1898*, which seems to be the first book on the subject, and in fact, on Coca-Cola collecting in general.

Because of the importance of trays, I find collectors have placed more emphasis on their condition than the condition of other pieces. The typical tray collector considers every little scratch and dent on a tray. That's why it is so difficult for a book like this to place values on trays, and I must stress, once again, that the prices you see here are just guides. In other words, they're average prices for clean, presentable trays (excellent or better condition). If a tray is rough, the price will be lower, and with more common trays, much lower. If the tray is in mint condition, the price

certainly can be higher. And just because a tray sells for a fortune at an auction, that doesn't mean that price is the true market value. It's very possible that two people just got carried away with the moment.

While it's quite possible that earlier trays do exist, the so-called 1897 "Victorian Girl" tray has always been thought of as the first and certainly the most important and most difficult to find of the trays. The earliest known trays, from 1897 through 1901, were 9¼" round. A 9¼" round tray was also used in 1903 in addition to a larger oval tray.

In 1905, The Coca-Cola Company produced a smaller oval tray. This seemed to have continued until 1909 with a series of medium and larger oval trays. Tip or change trays varied from 4" to 6" circular types until 1907, when they became standard 4¼" x 6" ovals until 1920, after which they were no longer produced.

Beginning in 1910, a rectangular tray was made, measuring 10½" x 13¼". It became standard and was used into the early 1960s. Between 1910 and 1919, rectangular trays were produced only in 1910, 1913 and 1914. In 1916, a completely different tray was produced measuring 8½" x 19". Subsequently, no trays were made until after World War I. Then, in 1920, production resumed on a regular basis, with at least one tray each year until 1942, and then no more until after World War II.

Most of these rectangular trays have appeared in sufficient numbers to keep collectors happy. However, most collectors strive for a mint or at least a near-mint example, neither of which is easy to find.

After World War II and into the 1950s and 1960s, the production of trays was, at best, spotty and irregular. TV trays, plastic trays, and commemorative trays replaced the popular and beautiful Coca-Cola girls of the 1920s and 1930s.

Displaying trays has always been a minor problem with collectors. Everything from magnets, plate hangers, and glue and string have been used, some successfully, while others not. I personally think the best way to display a tray is to lean it on a narrow shelf with a lip.

However you display your trays, it's essential to protect them. The most important thing is to avoid humidity. Don't store or display trays in a damp area such as game room or bar in a basement unless you use a dehumidifier, or they will gradually become pitted.

The other big problem with trays is dust. It always seems to accumulate on the bottom rim of the tray. If this dust is allowed to build up, it will be difficult to clean and could certainly detract from the tray. If trays are not cleaned and dusted properly, you will create a series of light scratches. With all of these warnings, I am trying to stress the fact that you must take care of your trays if you want to retain their value.

Whether you simply collect particular trays that strike your fancy, or you strive to own every example known, the serving tray is a classic Coca-Cola collectible.

Condition plays a crucial role in value! Items in this book are priced based on a condition rating of "excellent" or "8" (see page 22 for Condition Guide). Items in mint condition, or "10," could be worth more than the listed price, while items in fair or poor condition could be worth much less. Every flaw must be taken into consideration. Even rare examples in poor condition will have much less value than those shown in this book.

The items shown in this chapter are just a cross-section of the vast amount of memorabilia that Coca-Cola has produced. This sampling, however, should give you a good idea of what is available and their general values.

Exact size and dates have been indicated where possible. Many, however, are estimates.

Serving Trays

c. 1896, Ideal Brain Tonic brass plate, 10⅞", very rare $15,000

This embossed brass plate pre-dates tin litho. serving trays used by Coca-Cola. The exact use of this plate is unknown, but was probably used as a service plate or back bar piece. The debossed Coca-Cola logo in the center of the plate was originally covered in red enamel. Remnants of the enamel can still be seen throughout the logo.

1897, 9¼" ....$30,000   **1899**, 9¼" $20,000

1901, 9½" **$8,000**

1903, 9¼" **$7,000**

1903, 15" x 18½" **$10,000**

1903, 9¾", bottle tray..............................**$12,000**

1905, 10½" x 13", with glass $5,000

1906, 10½" x 13¼".........$5,000

1907, 10½" x 13¼", medium oval.........$4,000

1907, 13½" x 16½", large oval $8,500

c.1908, 12¼", "Topless Tray".....................$7,500

1909, 10½" x 13¼", medium oval.........$3,000

1909, 13½" x 16½", large oval...................**$4,500**

1913, 12¼" x15½".......................................**$850**

1914, 12½" x15¼".......................................**$650**

1910................. **$2,000**

1913.................... **$1,000**

1914...**$900**

1921..**$1,200**

1922..**$950**

1923..**$550**

1924, red (maroon) rim **$1,300**

1924, brown rim **$850**

1925...**$575**

1926...**$1,000**

1928, fountain sales....................................**$950**

1928, bottle sales.....................................**$1,000**

1929, bottle sales..**$750**

1929, fountain sales......................................$600

1930, fountain sales......................................$550

1930, bottle sales..$600

1931..$1,000

1933...**$850**

1934...**$1,000**

1935...$500

1936...$500

1937...$375

1938...$300

1939..$375

1941..$400

1942..$400

1950-52, screened background.......................$85

1950-52, solid background...........................**$250**

1953-60...**$65**

1957...**$300**

1958..**$40**

1961..**$30**
At least three versions were made.

Tip/Change Trays

1901, 6" **$3,500**

1901 variation, 5⅝" **$4,500**

1903, 6" **$2,000**

1903, 4"...$3,500

1903, 5½", bottle tray............................$10,000

1907, 4½" x 6" $1,000

1909, 4½" x 6" **$750**

1910, 4½" x 6" **$800**

1913, 4½" x 6"
....................**$700**

1916, 4½" x 6" **$285**

1914, 4½" x 6"
....................**$350**

Vienna Art Plates

Framed...$2,500
Without frame $850

Framed...$550
Without frame $275

Framed...$675
Without frame $350

Framed...$1,000
Without frame $650

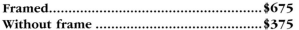

Framed..$675
Without frame $375

Framed $675
Without frame $350

Framed...$1,000
Without Frame...$700

Reverse side of art plate imprinted in center.
These plates can also be found with other or
no advertising on back. They have much less
value, and have nothing to do with Coca-Cola.

— Plates/Change Receivers —

c.1907, 7", change receiver, glass, The Empire Ornamental Glass Co., N.Y. **$2,500**

1931, 7¼", sandwich plate, E.M. Knowles China Co. **$400**

1969, frozen Coca-Cola change receiver, plastic
.... **$200**

Signs

Trolley Signs

Trolley cars, also called street cars, were first introduced in New York City in 1831. Originally, the trolleys were horse-drawn carriages that operated on tracks in the street. At the end of the 19th century, most major American cities built street railways, but it wasn't until electric street cars were introduced that street railways came into widespread use. The first electric trolley was installed in Richmond, Va., in 1887.

Unfortunately, because of the ever-growing popularity of the automobile, the street railway system began to decline and eventually die. But, in their time and because of their low cost and convenience, the trolleys were a popular form of public transportation and, therefore, an excellent place for companies such as Lucky Strike, Nabisco, and of course, The Coca-Cola Company, to target their advertising.

This advertising came in the form of cardboard signs, which collectors have dubbed "street car signs" or "trolley car signs." They are unmistakable because all are a standard size of 11" x 20-1/2", printed on a lightweight, flexible cardboard. The size of these signs was very important, because they were inserted into standard sized metal brackets, and the selling and changing of the signs was done by advertising agencies, many of which specialized in trolley advertising.

Young boys, hired by the ad agencies, usually changed the signs. One boy would stab the old sign with a sharp, pointed stick and lift it out with one swift motion. Another boy would follow and pick up the old signs. And yet another boy would insert new signs into the brackets. With the demise of the trolley as a major form of transportation, similar signs were used on buses and subways.

For collectors, trolley car signs have always been one of the most desirable and sought after of all Coca-Cola signs. Unfortunately, early ones are very rare. Because of the type of material they were made of and their exposure to the heat and the cold, trolley car signs are usually found in rough condition. Also, many of the signs are discolored because of smoke from smoking passengers.

Large Signs

Certainly the most difficult pieces to evaluate in a book such as this are large signs. Smaller versions are usually more appealing because most collectors lack sufficient room for displaying the larger ones. Displayability is the highest priority for most collectors, who believe they can use space better by showing a number of smaller signs than one large one. Consequently, the value of large signs will vary much more than their smaller counterparts. Personally, I'm not interested in 5-foot, 6-foot, or 8-foot signs at any price. I don't collect them, nor do I have a good market for selling them.

On the other hand, dealers and collectors who supply restaurants and taverns with these signs for decoration have a good market and will pay well for them. So unless you can find the right buyer, selling a larger sign is sometimes a real problem. I have received many letters and calls over the years from frustrated collectors who can't understand why they can't find a buyer for their 6- or 8-foot porcelain sign.

Therefore, before buying such a sign, ask yourself a few questions: Do I have the space to display this piece? Do I have the patience to find the right buyer? Do I also realize this sign will not appreciate in value like the smaller signs? Also keep in mind that the values shown are based on collector desirability for such signs.

Kay Displays

Beginning in 1934, Kay Displays, Inc. of New York City, produced signs and advertising displays for The Coca-Cola Company. Although the stamping on the back of many of these signs state "Designed & Manufactured by Kay Displays, Inc.," the company only designed the displays and didn't actually manufacture them. The owner and president of the company had a good working relationship with American Seating Co., of Grand Rapids, Mich. American Seating was an ideal partner for Kay Displays because it was able to produce the quantity and quality required by The Coca-Cola Company.

Before World War II, Kay and American Seating used various materials such as embossed lithographed tin, stamped metal, ornate cutout tin, wood, cardboard, and composition material. But with the approach of the war and constant demand for metal, display advertising was limited to material that would not interfere with the arms buildup.

Many of the Kay Designs produced from Dec. 7, 1941, to the end of the war reflected the patriotism and unity that swept the country. A pair of spread wings with a raised hand and bottle emblazoned many of the signs of this period and are among the most desirable of all Kay creations.

With the war over and the metal once again available, Kay's specialty signs took a back seat to the quickly produced, inexpensive, and long-lasting tin signs that The Coca-Cola Company was again using by the millions. Consequently, Kay Display went out of business in 1951, but it will live on forever in the hearts and collections of the individuals who appreciate its contribution to Coca-Cola advertising.

Condition plays a crucial role in value! Items in this book are priced based on a condition rating of "excellent" or "8" (see page 22 for Condition Guide). Items in mint condition, or "10," could be worth more than the listed price, while items in fair or poor condition could be worth much less. Every flaw must be taken into consideration. Even rare examples in poor condition will have much less value than those shown in this book.

The items shown in this chapter are just a cross-section of the vast amount of memorabilia that Coca-Cola has produced. This sampling, however, should give you a good idea of what is available and their general values.

Exact size and dates have been indicated where possible. Many, however, are estimates.

Paper Signs

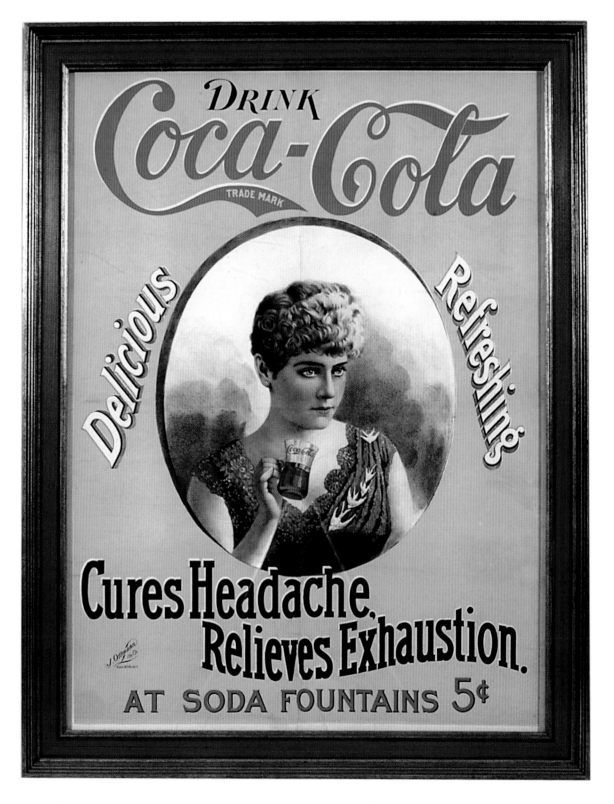

c.1896, 30" x 40", cameo paper sign, printed by J. Ottman Litho., Co., N.Y..................... **$25,000**

Pre-1900 paper signs are very rare.

1902, 14¾" x 19½", bottle sales...................... **$17,000**

1901, 14½" x 19¼", "Girl with Yellow Roses" **$15,000**

Beware of repros of this piece. Original has "copyrighted 1898 Wolf & Co., Phila." on lower right corner. One repro has a signature on left corner of table and cross (+) mark or marks on chest or table.

1902, 14¾" x 19½", fountain sales................... **$16,000**

1903, 14¾" x 19½", Hilda Clark **$17,000**

1904, 14½" x 19½", Lillian Nordica, metal strip, rare **$15,000**

1908, 14" x 22", "Good to the Last Drop," metal strip top and bottom, very rare **$17,000**

1913, 18" x 24", "Which? Coca-Cola or Goldelle Ginger Ale," rare **$10,000**

Photo courtesy of Dave Baker

1912, 16" x 24", printed by Ketterlinus Co., Philadelphia, Pa.......................................**$5,000**

c. 1912, 16" x 22", printed by Ketterlinus Co., Philadelphia, Pa.......................................**$6,500**

1920s, 13" x 22", heavy paper **$1,800**

1920s, 29½" x 43", printed by The Forbes Lithograph Mfg. Co., Boston, Mass............................**$8,500**

Late 1940s, 36" x 52", Amsterdam **$350**

Trolley Signs

Trolley signs are cardboard and a standard size of 11" x 22½".

1910, featuring "The Coca-Cola Girl" by Hamilton King and printed by Wolf & Co., Philadelphia, Pa. **$7,500**

1912... **$7,500**

c. 1912, "Whenever You See
An Arrow" **$2,000**

c.1912 .... **$5,000**

1914 .... **$7,500**

c.1918 ....$5,000

c. 1913 ....$5,000

1914.......................................$5,000

1923, "The Four Seasons"..........................$3,000

c. 1927 ....$3,500

Cardboard Signs

Photo courtesy of Scott Rosenman

1896, 6½" x 10½", hanging sign, cardboard
.... **$20,000**

Photo courtesy of the Brinker Collection

1905, 26" x 46", Lillian Nordica, rare **$15,000**

1909, 28½" x 45", cardboard sign, rare **$16,000**

1921, 18" x 30", paper sign **$2,500**

1928, 21½" x 32", "Girl with Bottle" **$2,800**

1920s, 10" x 14", "Hot Dog" **$2,800**

Late 1920s, 10" x 20", "Designed and Printed in Canada" (lower left) **$1,700**

1929, 19" x 31"..$2,000

1920s, 11" x 14" $400

1930s, 18" x 34" .... **$900**   **1938**, 14½" x 32" .... **$575**   **1938**, 21" x 44" **$500**

1935, 13" x 21", two-sided hanging sign **.......$750**   **1935**, 13" x 21", two-sided hanging sign **.......$800**

1936, 29" x 50", 50th Anniversary **$3,000**

1938, 34" x 50", "Girl with Roses," inside store display **$3,000**

1936, 27" x 56", rare **$3,600**

1936, 12½" x 33", litho. in Canada **$750**

1938, 29" x 50", signed Sundblom, printed by Niagara Litho., Buffalo, N.Y. **$3,000**

1938, 24" x 32", England **$2,100**

1939, 29" x 50" **$3,000**

1948, 31" x 45" **$800**

1940s, 29" x 50" $950

1946, 29" x 50"..................$700

1948, 29" x 50"...............$1,000

1956, 29" x 50", "Travel Girl".. $550

1942, 29" x 50", "Snowman," Niagara Litho. **$750**

1942, 29" x 50", "Two Girls at Car," Edwards & Deutsch Litho..... **$1,000**

1944, 16" x 27", with gold wood frame **$1,200**

1943, 16" x 27", with original frame **$1,000**

1940s, 16" x 27" ....$1,200   **1940s**, 16" x 27" $1,200

1942, with ornate wood frame, rare $3,000

1942, 16" x 27", "Umbrella Girl," Snyder & Black
.... **$650**

1941, 16" x 27"........ **$1,000**

1940, 16 x 27".. **$600**

1946, 16" x 27".....................**$700**

1942, 16" x 27", "Girl in Rain," Snyder & Black **$800**

1941, 16" x 27", "Girl Skater," Niagara Litho. Co....................**$650**

1941, 16" x 27".................................**$600**

1947, 16" x 27".............**$800**

1942, 16" x 27", "Young Couple," McCandlish Litho. **$600**

1946, 16" x 27"...**$600**

1948, 16" x 27"...**$500**

1955, 16" x 27"...**$400**

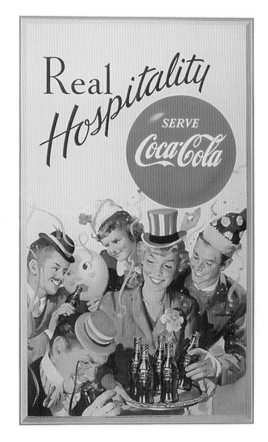

1952, 16" x 27"...**$400**

1945, 16" x 27" **$600**

1948, 16" x 27" **$600**

1948, 16" x 27" **$500**

1952, 16" x 27", with gold wood frame **.........$750**

1954, 16" x 27".......................... **$400**

1957, 16" x 27", "Snowman," with gold wood frame.................... **$600**

1949, 16" x 27".......................... **$400**

1940, 16" x 27".......................... **$450**

1952, 16" x 27".......................... **$400**

1952, 16" x 27".......................... **$300**

1950, 16" x 27".......................... **$400**

1956, 16" x 27".......................... **$300**

1956, 16" x 27".......................... **$400**

1939, 27" x 56"...**$2,400**

1941, 20" x 36", with original gold wood frame
....**$1,500**

1943, 20" x 36" with rare version of gold wood frame **$1,200**

1944, 20" x 36", with gold wood frame **$1,200**

1940s, 20" x 36", with gold wood frame **$1,500**

1941, 29" x 56" **$1,000**

1941, 20" x 36"..**$800**

1944, 20" x 36", with gold wood frame **$1,200**

1946, 20" x 36", "Yes Girl" award cardboard sign in
original wood frame **$1,600**

1942, 27" x 56", McCandlish, Litho. **$750**

1942, 27" x 56", "Picnic Grill," Snyder & Black.. **$750**

1940, 27" x 56", with original gold wood frame **$1,800**

1940s, 20" x 36", with gold wood frame....... **$950**

1944, with gold wood frame **$1,000**

1948, 20" x 36", with gold wood frame **$850**

1945, 20" x 36", with original gold wood frame **$850**

1945, 20" x 36", with original gold wood frame **$750**

1948, 23½" x 41" **$650**

1949, 20" x 36" **$800**

1938, 20" x 36"..**$850**

1948, 20" x 36"...**$450**

1953, 20" x 36", with original gold wood frame
....**$1,200**

1942, 20" x 36", with original gold wood frame
....**$800**

1942, 20" x 36"...**$750**

1950, 20" x 36"...**$600**

1950s, 20" x 36" $400

1957, 20" x 36", "Me Too," with aluminum frame **.. $750**

1950, 20" x 36", with gold wood frame $850

1950s, 20" x 36" $600

1952, 20" x 36"..$500

1956, 20" x 36"..**$400**

1950s, 20" x 36"..**$300**

1950s, 27" x 56", with aluminum frame **$450**

1960s, 20" x 36", with original aluminum frame
....**$225**

1958, 27" x 56"..**$350**

1960s, 27" x 56" **$225**

1950s, 27" x 56", in gold wood frame **........$3,500**

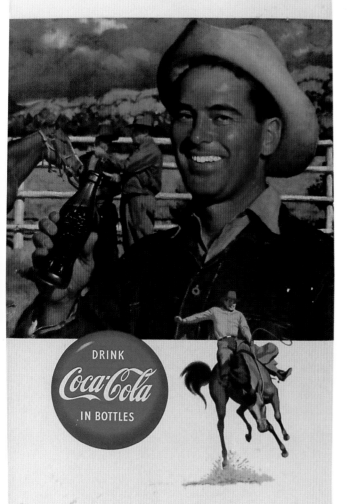

Talk about Good

DRINK
Coca-Cola
IN BOTTLES

1956, 20" x 36"................................$300

DRINK
Coca-Cola

ALWAYS REFRESHING,
THAT'S WHY THINGS
GO BETTER WITH COKE
AFTER COKE
AFTER COKE

1960s, 16" x 27", in aluminum frame
......................$225

for **extra fun**
take **more than one**

take an **extra carton** of **Coke**

in the
KING
size

DRINK
Coca-Cola

1960s, 16" x 27"..................................$50

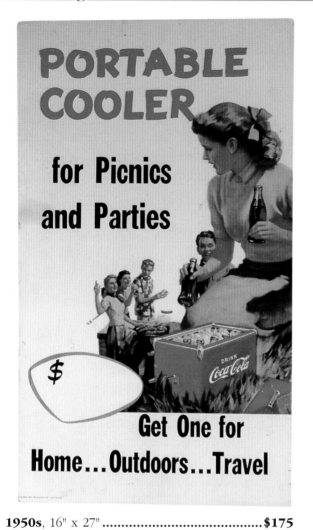

1950s, 16" x 27" $175

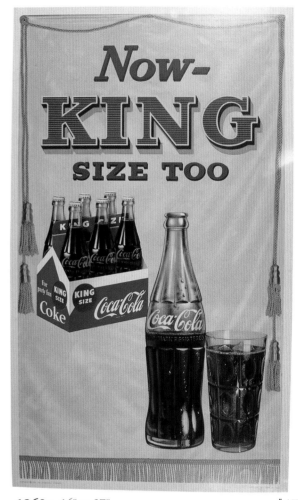

1960s, 16" x 27" $175

1957, 12" x 14" $275

1953, Sweetwater Clifton...... **$700**

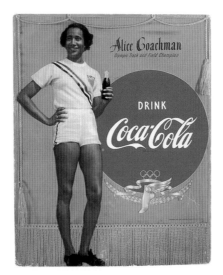

1953, Alice Coachman **$700**

1953, Sugar Ray Robinson.... **$750**

1953, Ted Rhodes................ **$450**

1953, Jesse Owens **$1,000**

1953, Buddy Young............. **$600**

1949..**$600**

1949..**$600**

1949...$600

1949...$650

1949...$600

1950s, 12" x 15", in aluminum frame **$700**

1950s, 12" x 15", in aluminum frame **$700**

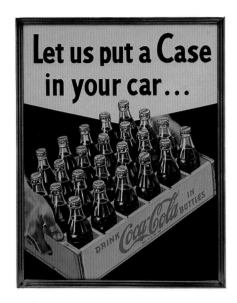

1950s, 12" x 15", in aluminum frame
.... **$500**

1950s, 12" x 15", in aluminum frame **$500**

1956, 15" x 16", two-sided
.... **$325**

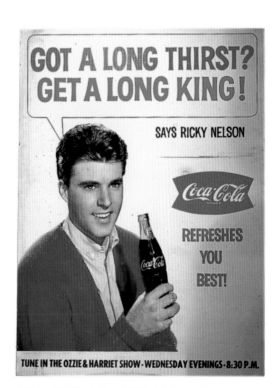

1959-1960, 14" x 18½", Ricky Nelson
.... **$700**

General Cutouts

c.1890s, 5½" x 8½", display piece, easel back, Wolf & Co., Phil., Pa...$7,000

c.1890s, 6½" x 7", display piece, easel back $8,000

1902, 8", hanging sign **$7,500**

1908, 14¾", "Cherub," hanging sign

.... **$6,000**

This cherub was produced in two types: hanging type shown to the right and easel-back stand up.

1906, 8½" x 11", cardboard hanging sign
.... **$10,000**

c.1909, 5' x 6', foldout window display, very rare when found complete **$16,000**

1910, 28½" x 39½", "Man in the Grass" (with glass), printed by American Lithography **$7,500**

This cutout also exists in a bottle version.

c.1912, 30" x 46", "Soda Fountain," window display, cardboard cutout **$10,000**

Photo courtesy of Gordon Jakway

c.1912, 29" x 38", "All the World"............. **$8,500**

1913, 30" x 35", "Couple at the Beach" (with glasses)
.... **$8,000**

This cutout also exists in a bottle version.

c.1911, 29" x 36", "Sundial" **$8,500**

c. 1918, 18" x 27", printed by
Ketterlinus, Philadelphia, Pa.
.... **$7,500**

c.1917, paper die-cut, part of a set of window trim..... **$2,500**

1924, 24" x 40"...$8,000

1916, 28" x 42" **$6,000**

1930, 18" x 42"......................................$2,200

1926, 28" x 42" **$4,500**

c.1926, 17" x 29¾", 3-D die-cut, rare, must be complete **$5,000**

c.1903, 4½" x 10½", cardboard sign, easel back, embossed, die-cut, Kaufman & Strauss Co., N.Y. **$16,000**

Photo courtesy of Chuck Campbell

c.1903, 4½" x 10½", cardboard sign, easel back, embossed, die-cut **$16,000**

1922, 32" x 40", "Girl on Aqua Plane," fold-out window display **$8,500**

1925, 15" x 20", cameo, easel back display **$2,000**

1925, 23" x 33", "People at Soda Fountain," fold-out window display **$1,600**

1920s, "Dahlia," window display fold-out, art from a painting by Carle Blenner **$850**

1937, 8½" x 14", Canada **.......** **$850**

1939, 12" x 16", (French) Canada
.... **$350**

1932, Dorothy Mackaill, easel
back, Niagara Litho Co. **$1,500**

1932, Loretta Young, easel back,
Niagara Litho Co. **$1,500**

1927, 16" x 28", soda jerk **$1,200**

1934, 48½", window display, Jackie Cooper and Wallace Beery **$4,500**

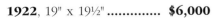

1922, 19" x 19½" **$6,000**

1926, 18" x 32", "Umbrella Girl," with bottle **$3,000**

1933, 25½" x 35½", window display **$5,500**

1931, 19" x 27", Norman Rockwell Art, shown incomplete (dog missing)..........................**$2,500**

1927, 13" x 30", "Circus Girl" **$750**
This piece is actually part of the circus window display.

1935, 18" x 36", Norman
Rockwell Art, printed by Snyder
& Black **$3,800**

1940s, 23" x 31", easel back $700

1944, 62½", "Woman Shopper"
display $1,000

1944, 15" x 19", cardboard cutout
display (Niagara Litho), 3-D hanging
or stand-up (another Sprite Boy
version exists), rare $2,700

1951, 15" x 18"..............................**$500**

1951, 14½" x 17"...**$450**

1951s, 14½" x 17".......................................**$450**

1944, 14" x 32"...**$1,200**

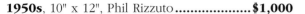

1950s, 10" x 12", Phil Rizzuto...................**$1,000**

1930s, 13" x 15", Germany..........................**$450**

1950s, 12" x 18" **$125**

1951, 18" x 26"...**$300**

1956, 18" x 19"...**$425**

1947, display sign.....**$135**

1950, 7" x 7", string hanger
.................................**$35**

1940s, 32" x 50" **$750**

1950s, 36" x 60", "Cowboy," mechanical point of purchase display, hands and eyes move **$1,800**

1962, 16" x 27", mechanical window display **$550**

c.1963, 15" x 30", easel back display **$375**

Festoon Cutouts

The values listed on festoon sets are based on complete examples in excellent condition. Incomplete sets will be priced much lower, while mint examples of complete sets in original envelopes will be priced higher.

1914, "North South East West" (shown without end pieces), rare...**$18,000**
Complete, very rare...................................**$23,000**

c.1918, "Umbrella Girls"
.... **$6,500**

1920s, "Lantern" festoon, rare **$7,500**

1930s, "Icicles," (five pieces) $1,000

1946, "Bathing Girls," (five pieces) $2,500

1950s, "State Birds" (five pieces)...............$1,200

1932, "Verbena"...**$3,000**

1960, "Birthstones" **$1,000**

1950s, "Know Your State Tree" **$575**

1951, "Girls Heads," (five pieces) hanging type **$1,700**

1951, "Girls Heads," (five pieces) standing type, easels on back **$2,200**

1951, "Market," (nine pieces) backbar display **$1,500**

Santa Cutouts

1941, 32" x 42", Santa window display **$1,500**

1946, 6" x 12" **$385**

1954, 10½" x 19" **$325**

1953, 9" x 18" **$375**

1962, 32" x 47"..**$425**

1950s, 36", easel back.................................**$275**

1949, 15", easel back **$375**

1950s, 18" x 27", 3-D **$200**

1948, 7½" x 13½" **$475**

1955, 19", easel back **$100**

Bottle Displays

1929, 7" x 9¾", "Winter Girl," bottle topper **$3,200**

1926, golfing couple, three-bottle display ...**$4,500**

1923, "Bottle Displays," cardboard cutouts, American Litho., N.Y. ..... **$1,000 each**
Complete set of four..**$5,000**

1920s, 10" x 14", "Boy with Weiner," cardboard cutout **$3,500**

1938, (French) Canada, cardboard cutout ..**$1,000**

1940, 21" x 40", carton display, 3-D cutout, actual six-pack slides under hand **$1,100**

1950s, bottle topper, plastic
....**$1,000**

1936, six-pack display............**$775**

"**6 for 25¢**"..........................**$550**

1950s, cardboard fold-up bottle display **$45**

1950s, (France), two bottle display, metal **$600**

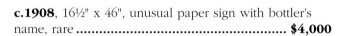

c.1908, 16½" x 46", unusual paper sign with bottler's name, rare **$4,000**

1950s, *Eddie Fisher* and *Kit Carson* TV shows, 34" x 68", canvas **$200**

1914, 18" x 48", canvas **$2,000**

1950s, 18" x 60", paper **$450**

1960s, 19" x 34", paper **$125**

1950s, 36" x 66", coin coolers, canvas **$300**

1951, 11" x 22", paper **$125**

1944, 8" x 25", Sprite Boy, paper **$350**

1950, 11" x 24", paper **$250**

1950s, 11" x 22", paper...................................**$85**

1954, 11" x 22", paper **$125**

1950s, 13" x 41", paper...................................**$85**

1952, 11" x 22", paper **$100**

1950s, 6" x 24", paper **$35**

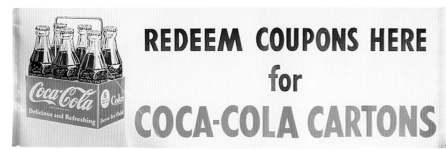

1950s, 7" x 22", paper **$60**

1899, 20" x 28", Hilda Clark, embossed tin, rare.......................................$20,000

c.1908, 12" x 36", Spanish **$2,000**

1930s, 5¾" x 17¾", embossed tin........................ **$375**

1931, 20" x 27"... **$1,000**

1914, 31" x 41", "Betty," self-framed tin.............. **$7,500**

1930s, 20" x 28" **$750**

1931, 20" x 27", embossed tin (in bottles variation)
....**$1,000**

1929, 20" x 28", "Gas Today," embossed tin **$3,000**

1934, 19" x 28"...................**$800**

1940s, 20" x 28", also made in masonite.............................**$450**

1927-1929, 7¾" x 30", diecut arrow...........**$1,000**

1922, 6" x 23" **$400**

1941, 20" x 28"..**$650**

1941, 20" x 28"..**$650**

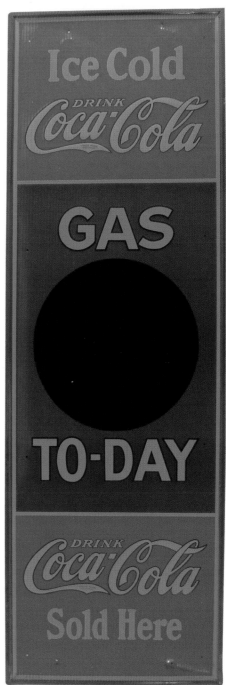

1931, 18" x 54"....................**$2,800**

1939, 19" x 28"...**$325**

1939, 19" x 28"...**$500**

1950s **$1,600**

1960s, 18" x 54" **$400**

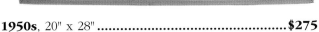

1950s, 20" x 28" **$275**

1963, 20" x 28" **$275**

1950s, 16" x 50" **$700**

1964, 11" x 28" **$275**

1950s, 20" x 28" **$450**

1950, 19" x 28" **$400**

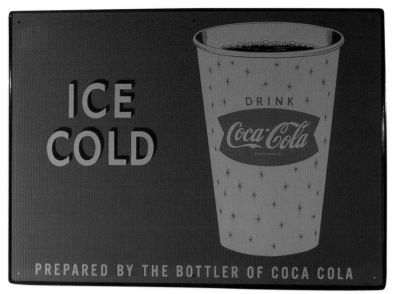

1963, 20" x 28"... **$375**

1950, 16" x 40".**$1,000**

c.1959, 18" x 53", rare
.........................**$1,700**

1948, 16" x 40"....**$425**

1964, 18" x 54"............. **$450**

1963, 18" x 54"...**$300**

1963, 9" x 12" **$100**

1963, 20" x 28" **$425**

1963, 84" **$950**

Flange and Tin Cutout Signs

1936, 16", 50th Anniversary, embossed tin **.........** **$2,500**

1950s, 11" x 12", six-pack sign **$950**

1950s, 11" x 12", six-pack sign **$950**

1950s, 16", tin **$385**

1939, flange sign $650

c. 1948-50, flange sign $800

1960s, flange sign $300

Porcelain Signs

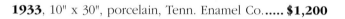

1933, 10" x 30", porcelain, Tenn. Enamel Co..**..... $1,200**

c. 1939, 14" x 27", masonite **$900**
Porcelain version.. **$1,500**

c. 1950s, 28" x 28", porcelain, made in both one-sided and two-sided versions **...... $1,500**

1949, 12" x 29", porcelain $525

c. 1950s, 12" x 18", porcelain $525

1950s, 12" x 28", "Fountain Service".........................$625

1948, 18" x 57", Canada **$1,600**

1952, 12" x 29", Canada, porcelain...............**$550**

c. 1950, 16" x 16", Canada, die-cut porcelain flange
....**$2,500**

c. 1950, 12" x 28", porcelain........................**$650**

1950s, 16" x 22", England, porcelain **$1,000**

Button and Disc Signs

1950s, 16", button sign with arrow, white, rare ..**$2,000**

1950s, 16", with aluminum arrow **$1,000**

1952, 10" x 36", wood and masonite with 12" disc **$1,000**

1950s, 24"...**$750**

1950s, 24"...**$450**

1950s, 16", German porcelain.............................**$500**

1950s, 16" x 40", with bottle **$1,000**

1950s, button calendar sign **$450**

1950s, spinner for top of vending machine **$1,200**

Glass Signs

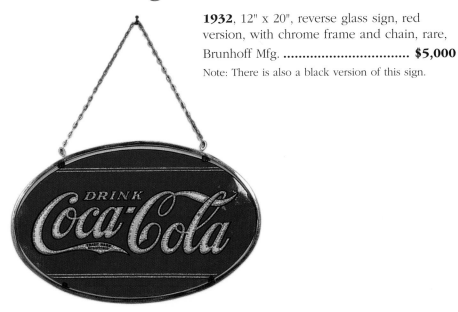

1932, 12" x 20", reverse glass sign, red version, with chrome frame and chain, rare, Brunhoff Mfg. **$5,000**

Note: There is also a black version of this sign.

1937, 10" x 12", reverse glass, foil back, metal frame **$5,500**

c.1937, 10" x 12", reverse glass, foil back, metal frame **$5,500**

1948, glass with wood base **$800**

1920s-mid 1930s, 11¼" dia., reverse glass mirror sign, ...**$575**

1950s, 10" dia., Germany, reverse glass sign, beveled edge, ...**$950**

1950, reverse glass sign on wood base................**$750**

1949, 18" x 22", reverse glass hanging sign, two-part, Price Bros. **$2,000**

1930s, 30", wood cutout **$3,000**

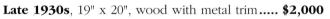

Late 1930s, 19" x 20", wood with metal trim**..... $2,000**

1939, wood and aluminum **$900**

── Miscellaneous Signs ──

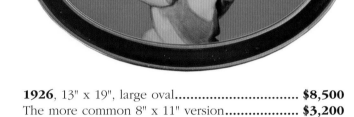

1907, 8" x 10", celluloid, manufactured by Whitehead
and Hoag Co., Newark, N.J. **$20,000**

The celluloid "Satisfied" sign is very rare. The price range is for
examples in high quality collector condition and complete with
ornate corners as shown. Examples in lesser condition will be
valued much lower.

1926, 13" x 19", large oval............................. **$8,500**
The more common 8" x 11" version.................. **$3,200**

1927, 8½" x 11"... **$950**

1920s, 6" x 12", hanging sign, celluloid **$1,800**

1922, 4" x 8", tin, embossed **$750**

1920s, 4½" x 12", tin over cardboard **$750**

1931, 4½" x 12½", tin, embossed **$650**

1930s, cooler sign, white porcelain with black trim **$950**

1930s, bottle-shaped aluminum door handle $450

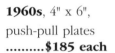 

1960s, 4" x 6", push-pull plates ....$185 each

1930s, Canada, porcelain push plates ....$400 each

1939, wood and masonite $400

1963, tin calendar holder $550

1964, tin calendar holder
.... **$400**

1970s, tin calendar holder
.... **$150**

1930s, 12½", composition, Kay Displays
.... **$1,800**

1930s, 7', tin and wood festoon, Kay Displays **$4,500**

Late 1930s, 12" x 30", wood hanging sign, Kay Displays
.... **$3,000**

Late 1930s, 10", decal bottle on embossed tin with cardboard back **$850**

Decal must be nice to warrant this value.

1940s, 9½" x 9½", wood, manufactured by Kay Displays **$200**

1940s, two-part wood hanging sign, manufactured by Kay Displays **$500**

c.1940s, 9", celluloid hanging sign **$350**

1950s, 10" x 12", pressed plastic easel back **$200**

c.1950s, 9", celluloid hanging sign, rare **$1,500**

c.1950s, 9", celluloid hanging sign **$300**

c.1941, 9½", stamped composition **$2,000**

c. 1939, arrow sign, wood and aluminum **$900**

1930s, 9" x 11", wood with metal trim, Kay Displays **$700**

Late 1930s, 11" x 39", wood cutout hanging sign, Kay Displays **$950**

1930s-40s, 10½" x 14", hanging sign, wood, Kay Displays **$1,000**

1930s, 2 part festoon, 12" x 32" (each), wood with metal trim, Kay Displays **$1,600**

1940s, two-part wood and tin hanging sign set............. **$1,200**
Each **$450**

1940s, menu board, wood with metal trim, shown with bottom piece missing ....**$475 as shown**

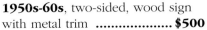

1950s-60s, two-sided, wood sign with metal trim **$500**

1930s, 25½", push bar, rare **$1,000**

1930s, 25½", push bar **$700**

1950s, door push bar, porcelain **$300**

1960s, 24", produced in many sizes **$400**

Thermometer Signs

c.1905, 5" x 21", wood **$650**

c.1905, 4" x 15", wood **$550**

c.1915, 5" x 21", wood **$600**

1950s, 8" x 36", porcelain **.. $1,500**

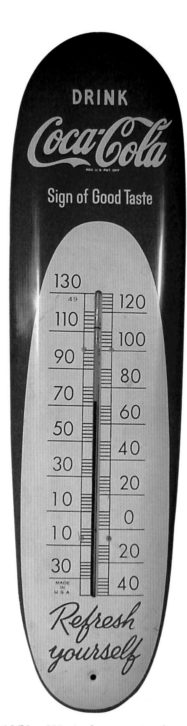

1950s, 30", tin (two versions)
....**$550**

1944, 7" x 17", masonite **....... $450**

1939, 6½" x 16", tin **............. $400**
Can be found with 1940 date.

1930s, 17", tin **..................... $500**

1936, 7" x 16", tin.................. **$400**   **1941**, 7" x 16", gold............... **$450**   **c. 1948**, 9" **$300**

1950s, 17", tin .... **$300**   **c.1939**, 9", tin................................**$2,200**

1950s, 8½" x 11", Germany, cardboard ...... **$150**   **1960s**, 4½" x 14", tin ...... **$200**   **1960s**, plastic **$100**

1950s, 12", glass front **$300**

1950s, 17", Canadian, tin   **$100**   **1957**, 12", glass front **$300**

— Light-Up Signs —

1920s, 18", leaded glass shade, "Chain Edge".... **$6,000**
"Property of The Coca-Cola Company - To Be Returned on Demand" appears twice on the top metal band.

1920s-1930s, milk glass globe with metal tassel **$2,500**

1930s, milk glass globe.................................... **$1,200**

1939, 15" x 20", neon hanging sign, rare **$5,500**

Late 1930s, 12" x 14", reverse glass, "The Brunhoff Mfg. Co.". **$5,000**

Late 1940s, 18" x 42", neon hanging sign **$1,700**

1950s, 17" x 17", plastic front, with cardboard insert **$650**

1950s, "Around the World," mechanical light-up sign, plastic front, rare **$3,000**

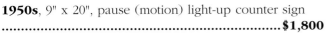

1950s, 9" x 20", pause (motion) light-up counter sign
....**$1,800**

1950s, 8" x 18", glass print, metal frame................**$500**

c.1960, 18" x 32", plastic light-up, rotating display,
shown complete...**$1,000**

1970s, 18" x 32", plastic light-up rotating display ...**$500**

Clock Signs

c. 1910, 4½" x 4½", gold stamped leather...**$3,000**

1930s, 5" x 9¼", cash-register-top sign/Sessions clock, Cincinnati Advertising Products, Cinncinnati, Ohio, rare **$4,500**

c. 1891-1895, Baird Clock **$7,000**

1901, Welch octagon schoolhouse clock with 1901 calendar insert as shown...**$8,000**
Without insert **$3,500**

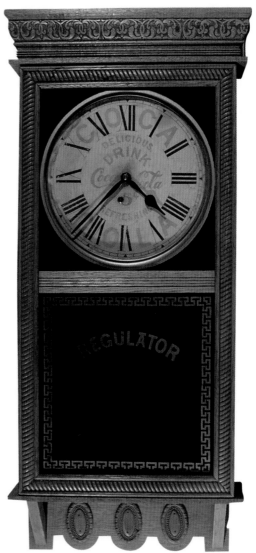

1910, Gilbert store regulator
..................................**$3,000**

1905-1907, Ingraham store regulator **$2,800**

1960s, desk clock.............................. **$100**

1930s, Gilbert store regulator
.... **$1,600**

c.1910, 3" x 8", leather desk
clock **$3,000**

c. 1939, 23", Spinner clock, neon, Electric Clock Co.,
Columbus, Ohio **$3,600**

1939/40, 17½", "Spinner" neon clock **$5,000**

1939-42, reverse glass, metal frame **$1,200**

1948, 36" **$800**

c.1948, 19"...................... **$650**

1950, glass-front light-up.. **$700**

1950s, glass front **$650**

1960s, glass front **$350**

1970s, plastic **$50**

1950s, metal **$650**

1950s, light-up glass front **$650**

1951, 17½", maroon.. **$250**

1951, 17½", silver **$275**

1960s, plastic **$175**

1960s, glass front **$400**

1960s, plastic **$200**

1970s, plastic light-up........**$100**

1970s, plastic **$100**

1970s, plastic digital **$100**

1970s, 16" x 20", plastic light-up **$185**

1970s, plastic **$60**

1980, Sessions, numbered limited edition presented by Coca-Cola USA for sales excellence **$700**

Bottles

Bottles have long been a favorite among collectors of Coca-Cola memorabilia. A fascinating variety of styles, shapes, and colors were used through the years, although most collections seem to focus on the various cities where Coca-Cola bottling franchises have existed.

The earliest bottles known to contain Coca-Cola were of the Hutchinson stoppered variety. The words Coca-Cola appear in either block print or script lettering on the bottles, and embossing usually designates the city where the bottle was originally filled. Hutchinson bottles were used only briefly and by fewer than a dozen bottling works just after the turn of the century. Relatively few have survived.

In the early 1900s, crown-top, straight-sided bottles replaced the heavier, cruder Hutchinson bottles. Millions of crown-top bottles were used by the ever-increasing number of Coca-Cola franchises between 1902 and 1915. Few records were kept, however, and individualism was rampant. A given Coca-Cola bottling works might have used bottles of several different styles and colors at various times. Some bottles had fancy designs such as rings, shields, or arrows embossed onto the glass; still others had slug plates identifying the then proprietor of the Coca-Cola franchise. Many straight-sided bottles displayed a paper label identifying the product they contained and bore the Coca-Cola trademark embossed in script lettering as well.

The early crown-top bottles were hand blown in molds, with their necks and lips finished by special hand-held tools. Such techniques often left rough seams, irregular patterns of thick and thin glass, numerous bubbles and imperfections in the glass itself, and sometimes crooked shapes. Machine-made crown-top bottles with fewer deficiencies and evenly formed seams began to replace the hand-tooled bottles after 1910. The variety of glass colors ranged from clear and aqua to differing shades of blue, green, and amber. Even the amount of liquid a bottle contained varied considerably since 6, 6½, 7, and up to quart-size 24- and 26-ounce bottles existed. The script writing Coca-Cola trademark sometimes appeared at the base of the bottle, sometimes in the center and sometimes on the shoulder. While this lack of uniformity creates interesting collections of straight-sided Coca-Cola bottles, the inevitable confusion generated by such diversity eventually led to the adoption of the now famous "hobbleskirt" or "Mae West" shaped bottle as the standard glass container for Coca-Cola shortly after 1915.

The first patent for hobbleskirt bottles was issued on Nov. 16, 1915, to the Chapman Root Glass company of Terre Haute, Ind. The patent was renewed on Dec. 25, 1923. Such "Thanksgiving" or "Christmas" Coke bottles, as they are sometimes called, have become quite popular among collectors because the base plate of most of these bottles bear the name of the city where they were first filled.

Well over 2,000 cities are known to have been home to Coca-Cola bottlers as the bottling network expanded. The classic shape has received several patent renewals since 1923, and hundreds of millions of hobbleskirt bottles were put into service over the years.

Many bottles can be found on which the words Coca-Cola or "property of Coca-Cola" appear in block letter print only. Although some of these bottles are of the older, hand-blown variety, most date from the 1920s or later. Collectors generally agree that these block letter bottles probably didn't contain Coca-Cola, but rather the various fruit-flavored drinks that were handled by individual bottling franchises. Often these bottles had paper labels identifying the kind of soda water they contained. Larger, quart-size bottles were also used this way.

These "block letter" bottles come in a variety of colors and shapes, and make for an interesting collection of their own. A surprising number have fancy embossings, such as people or animals. But very few, if any, were ever used for Coca-Cola, and the "flavor bottles" generally do not have the value of bottles that actually contained Coca-Cola.

Two other types of bottles deserve mention. Syrup bottles did indeed contain genuine Coca-Cola syrup obtained from the parent company in Atlanta and were used at sit-down soda fountains to hand-mix one's 5-cent drink

with carbonated water. Many of these tall, clear glass bottles have the words Coca-Cola in acid-etched lettering or printed on paper labels sometimes sealed under glass. The trademark appears on such bottles in block lettering or in script.

Certain Coca-Cola franchises also bottled and sold seltzer water to local outlets such as bars, restaurants, and soda fountains. This was done in a variety of beautifully colored or clear glass siphon bottles with acid-etched lettering or applied color labeling. The words Coca-Cola are found on these bottles in both block letter or script writing styles, although such bottles were used for seltzer water only and never to dispense Coca-Cola.

The relative value placed on Coca-Cola bottles is largely determined by the age of the bottle (Hutchinson, straight-sided, or hobbleskirt), its scarcity (small town versus franchise, for example), and the color of the glass and condition of the bottle (free from chips, cracks, cloudiness, and considerable wear). An original metal crown or paper label enhances the value of a bottle appreciably.

Condition plays a crucial role in value! Items in this book are priced based on a condition rating of "excellent" or "8" (see page 22 for Condition Guide). Items in mint condition, or "10," could be worth more than the listed price, while items in fair or poor condition could be worth much less. Every flaw must be taken into consideration. Even rare examples in poor condition will have much less value than those shown in this book.

The items shown in this chapter are just a cross-section of the vast amount of memorabilia that Coca-Cola has produced. This sampling, however, should give you a good idea of what is available and their general values.

Exact size and dates have been indicated where possible. Many, however, are estimates.

Hutchinson Bottles

Script, Jasper, Ala.
.... **$3,000**

Script, "Property of Coca-Cola" **$3,500**

Script, Birmingham, Ala.
.... **$2,500**

No mention of Coca-Cola, Biedenharn Candy Co. **$300**

— Amber Bottles —

c.1905, Philadelphia, Pa., with original paper label **......... $300**

Knoxville, Tenn. **............. $65**

— Clear/Light Green Bottles —

Muskogee, Okla. **........... $165**

Okmulgee, Okla., rare **.............$275**

Altus, Okla. **............... $125**

Hobbleskirt Bottles

1916-1924, embossed, "Bottle Pat'd Nov. 16, 1915"................. **$6 to $15**

1924-1937, embossed, "Bottle Pat'd Dec. 1923" (Christmas Coke)............ **$3 to $8**

1937-1948, embossed "Bottle Pat'd 105529," changed to "In U.S. Patent Office" in 1951 .... **$1 to $3**

1950s, ACL and embossed, "Contents 6½ Fluid Ozs." ....**$1 to $2**

1960s, ACL, "Coke" on reverse side .... **$.50 to $1**

— Diamond Design Bottles —

1960s, 10 oz., diamond............. **$5**

1960s, 10 oz., diamond, paper label
.... **$550**

1960s, diamond, foil label prototype
.... **$1,000**

1960s, diamond, foil label, rare
prototype....................... **$1,200**

1960s, Canada, 10 oz., plain
diamond **$35**

1960s, ACL, diamond............ **$250**

1960s, green glass, multi-diamond, paper label **$235**

1960s, multi-diamond, paper label **$125**

1960s, ACL, multi-diamond prototype **$150**

1960s, ACL, multi-diamond prototype............................ **$150**

1960s, ACL, 10 oz., "turn-top" cap......................... **$150**

1960s, ACL, New Zealand
.... **$275**

1960s, 16 oz., foil label, screw-top
.... **$150**

1960s, multi-diamond, screw top, quart **$55**

1960s, ACL, 12 oz. large mouth prototype, rare **$750**

1960s, 28 oz., multi-diamond, twist top **$65**

1960s, ACL, 1 pt. 10 oz., prototype........................ **$800**

1960s, ACL, 1 pt. 10 oz., prototype............ **$800**

1960s, ACL, multi-diamond, 1 pt. 10 oz., prototype............ **$750**

Seltzer/Syrup Bottles

Bradford, Pa. **$275**

Susanville, Calif. **$165**

1930s, glass syrup jug with paper label and original box.................... **$450**

Early 1900s, embossed glass syrup jug**.........** **$3,500**

1950s, syrup can**..** **$85**

Cans

1955, first production can, test market from New Bedford, Mass., for export to U.S. troops in the Far East **.......................................** **$750**

1959, test market can........... **$425**   **1960**, first domestic can ...... **$400**   **1960**, Canada **$175**

Note: These cans must be in mint (10) condition to warrant these prices.

1960s, Canada .... **$500**   **1961**, first bottle diamond
.... **$200**   **1963**, second bottle diamond
.... **$175**

1963, third bottle diamond... **$150**

1963, 7 oz. bottle diamond prototype, rare **$1,500**

1966, first multi-diamond **$65**

Note: These cans must be in mint (10) condition to warrant these prices.

1960s, second multi-diamond. **$35**

1960s, third multi-diamond, all-aluminum **$75**

Bottle Carriers

1924, six-pack carrier, cardboard
.... **$375**

1930s, six-pack carrier, cardboard................. **$650**

1940s, cardboard..**$125**

Mid-teens to 1930s, vendor's carrier with straw holder, tin...**$750**

1941, wood with bottle separators **.....** **$300**

1941, wood .... **$200**   **1940s**, wood/cardboard **$65**

Late 1940s, steel .... **$125**   **1950s**, aluminum **$125**

1930s, six-pack carrier, cardboard **$250**

c.1938, six-pack carrier, cardboard **$185**

c.1938, six-pack carrier, cardboard **$125**

1940s, six-pack carrier, wood, masonite...............................**$225**

1950s, six-pack carrier, aluminum **$200**

1930s, 12 bottle carrier, wood

1950s, six-pack carrier, cardboard..................................... **$25**

1940s, 12 bottle carrier, wood, rare...................**$400**

1950s, 12 bottle carrier, aluminum...................**$185**

1940s, wood.....................................**$85**

1950s, aluminum...**$200**

1950s, aluminum...**$135**

1950s, aluminum...**$100**

1950s, aluminum..$50

1950s, 12 bottle carrier, aluminum $125

1960s, four pack $8

1940s-1950s, vendor's metal bottle carrier $300

Coolers and Ice Chests

1940s, 17" x 22", table top ice chest, cooler, rare, small size
....**$2,500**

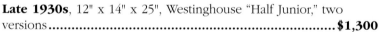

Late 1930s, 12" x 14" x 25", Westinghouse "Half Junior," two versions **$1,300**

1950s, cooler, France........... **$350**

1950s, picnic cooler, vinyl.. **$225**

Late 1940s, steel cooler box **$650**

1940s-1950s, airline cooler **$550**

1950s, Acton, 6 pack cooler **$300**

1964-65, World's Fair cooler box, vinyl $125

1960s, picnic cooler $125

1964, picnic cooler $175

Glasses and Related Items

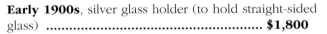

Early 1900s, silver glass holder (to hold straight-sided glass) **$1,800**

1900-1904, straight-sided glass.................... **$1,300**

1912-1913, small 5¢ flare glass **$1,000**

1914-1918, "Drink" flare glass........................ **$500**
Beware of reproductions.

1904, flare glass with syrup line
.... **$500**

1904, flare glass variation..... **$500**

1923-1925, modified flare glass
.... **$125**

c1927, modified flare
glass...................... **$125**

1930s, tin water cup............ **$150**

1929-1940, bell-shaped glass
.... **$40**

For the first 30 years or so of The Coca-Cola Company's existence, the product was aimed at adults. For example, the company used slogans such as "Relieves Fatigue," "The Ideal Beverage for Discriminating People" and "For Shoppers and Businessmen." It wasn't until the late 1920s and early 1930s that it considered youngsters an important market.

But when the company began catering to children, it did an admirable job. By far the most popular items in this section are the toy cars and trucks. But not all items in this section were produced with children in mind. Playing cards, for example, have always been an important "give-away" for adults.

Condition plays a crucial role in value! Items in this book are priced based on a condition rating of "excellent" or "8" (see page 22 for Condition Guide). Items in mint condition, or "10," could be worth more than the listed price, while items in fair or poor condition could be worth much less. Every flaw must be taken into consideration. Even rare examples in poor condition will have much less value than those shown in this book.

The items shown in this chapter are just a cross-section of the vast amount of memorabilia that Coca-Cola has produced. This sampling, however, should give you a good idea of what is available and their general values.

Exact size and dates have been indicated where possible. Many, however, are estimates.

General Toys and Games

1930s, Ideal "Wonder Doll" in original box with insert brochure, Coca-Cola on bottom of doll's shoes.
.... **$4,000**
This doll is rare; very rare with original box.

1950s, 12", Buddy Lee doll, plastic
.... **$1,200**

Close-up of baseball glove strap.

1930s, child's baseball glove, "Drink Coca-Cola in Bottles", rare **$700**

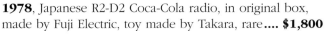

1978, Japanese R2-D2 Coca-Cola radio, in original box, made by Fuji Electric, toy made by Takara, rare**.... $1,800**

1980s, Cobot in original box **$200**

1930-31, "Coca-Cola Flyer" three-wheel scooter, 36" long**........ $2,500**

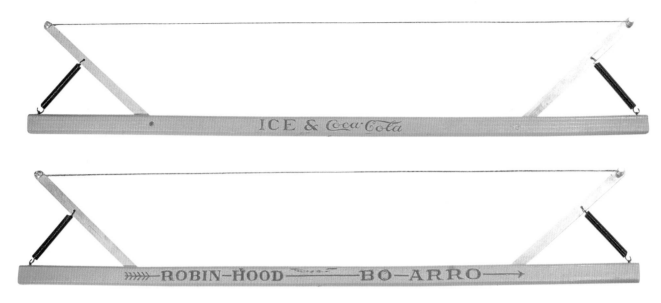

1930-31, Robin Hood BO-ARRO toy bow and arrow **$375**

1940s-50s, bingo set **$75**

Tick-Tac-Toe **$225**

1940s, bingo card **$40**

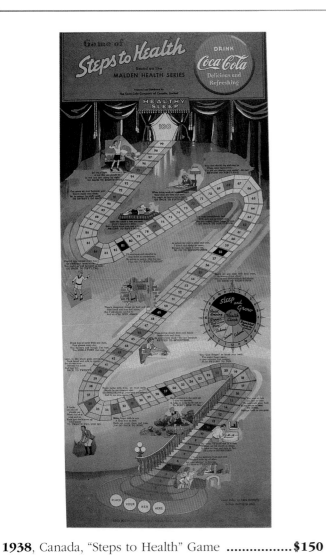

1940s, Dominos **$65**

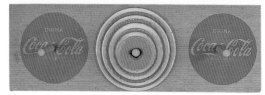

1938, Canada, "Steps to Health" Game **$150**

1949, Tower of Hannoi Game **$250**

1940s-50s, darts (darts not marked with logo) **$55**

1932, Olympic record indicator **$165**

1952 Puzzle, 12" x 18", Bill Gregg art, with original
envelope

English... **$400**
French, Canadian **$325**

1940s, "15" puzzle, wood.................................. **$225**

c.1959 puzzle, London with original box **$100**

c.1979 puzzle in a resealable can........................ **$25**

c.1916-1920, 5¾", cardboard whistle, shown open and closed **$750**

Miniatures, Radios, and Music Boxes

1939, salesman sample cooler with carrying case and complete set of inside pages **$4,000**

1929, Glascock salesman sample cooler, 8" x 10½" x 13" **$7,000**

1929, mint in original carrying case **$16,000**

1950s, "Dole Director," salesman sample dispenser with original carrying case.................. **$2,500**

1950s, 7" x 12" x 9½", cooler radio...............**$750**

This radio is not difficult to find, but must be working and in excellent condition with original knobs to justify this price.

1950s, 7" x 12" x 9½", Mexico, cooler radio....**$1,000**

1950, crystal radio set.....................................**$350**
Set with original instructions **$400**

1950s, cooler music box, different versions ... **$3,000**

1950, miniature cooler music box (working) ... **$225**

1970s, vending machine radio in original box **$300**

1950s, plastic vending machine bank....................**$250**

1950s, plastic toy dispenser in original box **$150**
Without box...**$65**

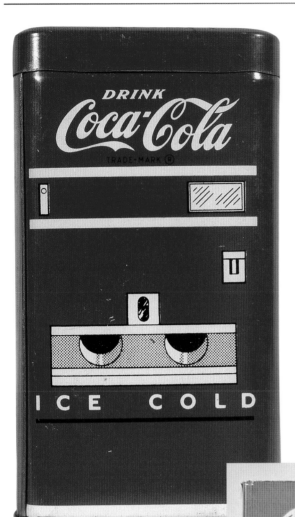

1950, 4" x 2¼", tin bank
.... **$135**

1960s, vending machine bank,
plastic **$125**
Bank in box........................ **$200**

1930s, miniature six pack **$225**

1930s, "Chatta-Box," mini 24-bottle wood case with bottles, rare **$400**

1950s, ceramic case...**$325**

1950s, plastic mini picnic cooler with bottles **$225**

Toy Trucks

c.1932, No. 171 Metalcraft truck, with rubber wheels
.... $1,200

c.1934, Metalcraft, long front, rubber wheels, rare
.... $3,600

1949-50, Goso tractor trailer, wind-up, very rare **..** $2,500

1950s, 5½", GMC truck $1,200

1948, Buddy-L, wood, rare $5,000

Early 1940s, Smith Miller, wood and metal, with wood
blocks $2,200

c.1949, Goso, rare **$3,500**

1950s, Marx, plastic **$900**

1950s, Marx, plastic **$900**

1950s, Marx, plastic **$1,000**

1950s, Marx, Sprite Boy **$1,100**

1950s, Marx **$1,800**

1950s-60s, battery operated, yellow and white **$550**

Early 1950s, 7", Marx truck **$600**

c.1954, Marx **$700**

1950s-60s, battery operated, red and white **$650**

1960s, Buddy-L **$475**

1948-1950, Italian, wood, tin, and Bakelite, very rare
.... **$4,000**

1950s, Marx No. 21 (Canadian version), very rare
.... **$1,500**

1959, Buddy-L, orange **$800**

Playing Cards

1909
.... **$6,000**

1928
.... **$1,200**

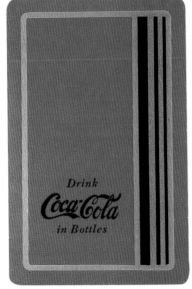

1936...**$600**

1938...**$400**

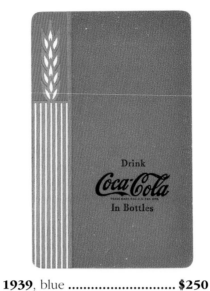

1938...................................... **$500**   **1939**, blue .... **$250**   **1943**...................................... **$125**

1943...................................... **$125**   **1943**...................................... **$125**   **1943**...................................... **$125**

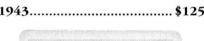

1943...................................... **$500**   **1943**...................................... **$500**   **1956**...................................... **$125**

1956.............................$125

1958.............................$145

1958.............................$100

1959.............................$100

1963.............................$100

1963.............................$85

1980s $20

Paper items include smaller advertising pieces like bookmarks, stamp holders, notebooks, postcards, fans, menus, and coupons. They are typically practical items that could be used around the home rather than the display items that simply were only for decoration and viewing. The Coca-Cola advertising executives were wise to offer these handy products, as they provided potential customers with constant exposure to their product, as people would read and reread the slogans as they went about their daily lives.

Condition plays a crucial role in value! Items in this book are priced based on a condition rating of "excellent" or "8" (see page 22 for Condition Guide). Items in mint condition, or "10," could be worth more than the listed price, while items in fair or poor condition could be worth much less. Every flaw must be taken into consideration. Even rare examples in poor condition will have much less value than those shown in this book.

The items shown in this chapter are just a cross-section of the vast amount of memorabilia that Coca-Cola has produced. This sampling, however, should give you a good idea of what is available and their general values.

Exact size and dates have been indicated where possible. Many, however, are estimates.

Bookmarks

1898, 2" x 2¼", bookmark, celluloid
.... **$700**

1900, 2" x 2¼", bookmark, celluloid
.... **$600**

c.1906, 1½" x 3⅛", "Owl" bookmark, celluloid **$800**

1904, 2" x 6", Lillian Nordica bookmark.............................. **$325**

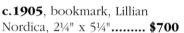

c.1905, bookmark, Lillian Nordica, 2¼" x 5¼"**........ $700**

c.1910, bookmark, celluloid, Mobile, Ala. **$800**

c.1910, bookmark, celluloid, Mobile, Ala.. .... **$800**

Stamp Holders, Note Pads, and Postcards

1900, 1½" x 2½", stamp holder with calendar, celluloid **$700**

1902, 1½" x 2½", postage stamp holder, celluloid **$650**

1903, 2½" x 5", Hilda Clark note pad, celluloid **$600**

1902, 2½" x 5", note pad, celluloid **$750**

1910, "The Coca-Cola Girl" post card, Hamilton King Art **$850**

1911, "Motor Girl" post card **$850**

Fans, Menus, and Coupons

c.**1894**, fan showing both sides, rare $4,000

1900, fan, showing both sides $325

1902, 4⅛" x 6⅛", menu **$900**

1904, 4⅛" x 6½", menu **$850**

Back of both menus.

1890s, coupon showing both sides, Wine Coca Co., Atlanta, Ga. **$1,200**

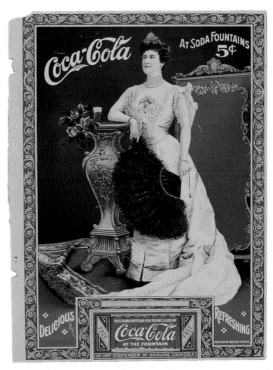

1901, 1⅝" x 3⅜", Hilda Clark "Free Drink" coupon **$900**

1905, 6½" x 9¾", "Lillian Nordica" magazine ad with coupon. **$325**
Beware of smaller size reproduction.

1905, 3¾" x 7", "Lillian Nordica" ad card with coupon, (front and back shown) **$900**
Rare when found complete. Coupon must be attached to warrant this price.

Trade Cards

c.1892, 3½" x 5½", trade card **$2,000**

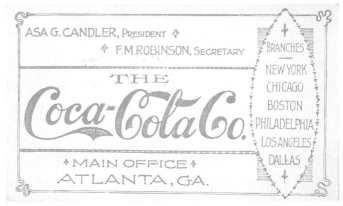

1901, 2¼" x 3⅞", trade card, rare **$1,700**

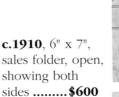

c.1910, 6" x 7", sales folder, open, showing both sides **$600**

c.1907, folding trade card, shown open and closed **$1,000**

— Miscellaneous Paper —

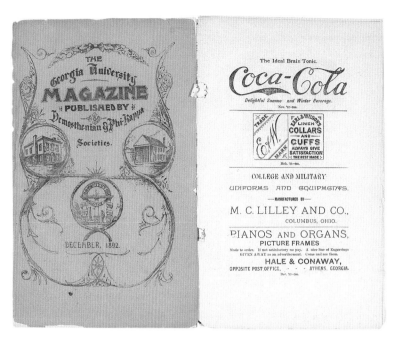

1892, Georgia University Magazine with Coca-Cola Ad **...... $375**

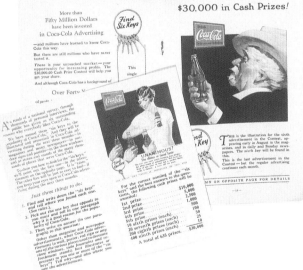

1927, booklet describing "Six-Keys" Contest **..... $25**

1930s, cigar bands (glass & bottle) **.................. $185 each**

The following is a complete set of 1936 Olympic Games Schedules, showing front and back of each. Individual folders are rare, and the complete set is very rare.

Each $300
Complete set.......................................$1,500

Each $300
Complete set.......................................$1,500

Each $300
Complete set...$1,500

Each $300
Complete set...$1,500

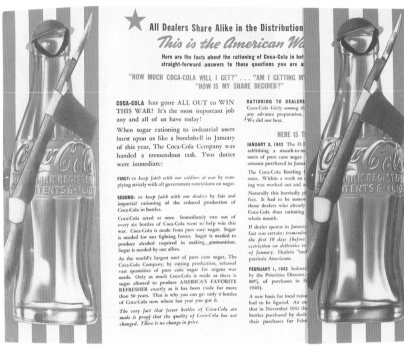

1941-42, 8½" x 17", paper folder recommending Coke for servicemen **$100**

1954, mini college pennant, order form with three pennants **$85**

1952, carton insert, Giants baseball, Wes Westrum

1953, carton insert, 3⅛" x 7⅛", Flash Gordon tee shirt offer **$200**

1964-65, 11" x 16½", N.Y. World's Fair Coca-Cola Pavilion Folder **.......$25**

Miscellaneous

The Coca-Cola Company has always been a leader in advertising. Early on, it showed a creativity that would put some modern companies to shame, even though modern firms have access to sophisticated resources like national marketing surveys, computer-generated statistical models, and high-tech television commercials with digitally enhanced graphics.

While the early Coca Cola company didn't have the wonderful resources we have today, it did make the most of what it had available at the time. Coca-Cola put its logo on almost everything imaginable. And, of course, licensing its name for use on other companies' products was mutually beneficial. The widespread presence of the Coca-Cola logo helped sell the drink, and in turn, the logo gave prestige and visibility to the products of lesser known companies.

Items in this section include figures, pocket mirrors, silverware, pocket knives, ink pens, letter openers, tools, jewelry, smoking paraphernalia, and convention badges.

Condition plays a crucial role in value! Items in this book are priced based on a condition rating of "excellent" or "8" (see page 22 for Condition Guide). Items in mint condition, or "10," could be worth more than the listed price, while items in fair or poor condition could be worth much less. Every flaw must be taken into consideration. Even rare examples in poor condition will have much less value than those shown in this book.

The items shown in this chapter are just a cross-section of the vast amount of memorabilia that Coca-Cola has produced. This sampling, however, should give you a good idea of what is available and their general values.

Exact size and dates have been indicated where possible. Many, however, are estimates.

3-D Objects

1930s, 6½" tall, "Salesman of the Month" statue
....**$800**

1950s, Sprite Boy napkin holder.......................**$1,300**

1930s, pretzel dish, aluminum.............................**$250**

1969, 14", frozen Coca-Cola stuffed doll...............**$150**

Pocket Mirrors

1906, The Whitehead & Hoag Co., Newark, N.J., Duplicate Mirrors 5¢ Postage, Coca-Cola Company, Atlanta, Ga............................ **$650**

1907, From the painting, copyright 1906, by Wolf & Co., Phila., Bastian Bros. Co., Roch., N.Y., Duplicate Mirrors 5¢ Postage, Coca-Cola Company, Atlanta, Ga. **$650**

1908, Bastian Bros. Co., Rochester, N.Y., Duplicate Mirrors 5¢ Postage, Coca-Cola Company, Atlanta, Ga. **$1,100**

1909, J.B. Carroll, Chicago, Duplicate Mirrors 5¢ Postage, Coca-Cola Company, Atlanta, Ga..... **$600**

1910, J.B. Carroll, Chicago, Duplicate Mirrors 5¢ Postage, Coca-Cola Company, Atlanta, Ga...... **$375**

1911, The Whitehead & Hoag Co., Newark, N.J., Duplicate Mirrors 5¢ Postage, Coca-Cola Company, Atlanta, Ga.............................. **$325**

1914, The Whitehead & Hoag Co., Newark, N.J. **$650**

1916, The Whitehead & Hoag Co., Newark, N.J. **$425**

1920, Bastian Bros. Co., Rochester, N.Y.. **$850**

1931, Spanish (So. American Market), The American Art Works, Inc. Coshocton, Ohio, rare **$3,500**

Small Items

c.1912, 1½" dia., watch fob, celluloid, showing both sides
.... **$3,200**

1920s, "Safe Driving Award" pin, enameled, rare.... **$500**

c.1910, watch fob, celluloid **$1,200**

1940s, 1¼" five year no accident pin **$100**

c.1905-1915, nickel silver, four blade knife **$600**

c.1913-1915, brass door knob **$600**

1947, 1¼" x 2½", belt buckle, sterling silver **$500**

c.1920, 4", hat pin, chromed **$300**

c.1920-1930, saber or sword opener, two different examples .... **$300 each**

c.1920, blotter pad, celluloid cover, Woodward, Okla. **$400**

1920s, silverware............. **$185 each**

1920s, notepad holder for candlestick phone
....**$400**

1930s, door lock in original box.....................**$85**

1950s, plastic night light in box
.... **$45**

1940s, 10" dia., sundial, bronze
.... **$3,000**

1950s, mechanical pencil
(bottle clip).......................... **$30**

1940s-50s, letter opener, chrome **$85**

c.1929, 12½" long, axe "For Sports Men," mint in original box $2,500

1930s, crowbar, Greenwood Coca-Cola Bottling Co. $450

1968 Olympics (Mexico), 4¼", pin tray, sterling silver sombrero, two gold applied plaques, Coca-Cola logo and Olympics logo $750

1963, bookends, bottle shaped, bronze $275

1950s, tie clip, enameled.......... $100

— Smoking Items —

c.1908, match safe, celluloid, made by Whitehead and Hoag, showing both sides, rare**............$4,000**

1912, matchbook showing both sides **................ $1,000**

1910, "The Coca-Cola Girl" matchbook, showing both sides **..$1,600**

1930s, brass matchbook holder **$125**

1950s, cigarette lighter **$185**

1960s, mini can lighter **$65**

1920s, matchbook **$40**

1940s, glass ashtray $75

1950s, glass ashtray $10

1950s, glass ashtray $25

1940s, bakelite ashtray....................................$70

1930s, "pullmatch" ashtray **$2,500**

1936, 50th Anniversary ashtray, porcelain, personally
signed at the 1936 convention, rare **$850**

1950s, ceramic ashtray..**$165**

1958, foil coasters

Each $7
Set of three $35

1958, foil coasters

Each $7
Set of three $35

1958, foil coasters

Each $7
Set of three $35

Convention Badges

1916, convention medal, porcelain inlay**.....$1,000**

c.1930, convention badge **$125**

1939, convention badge........ **$135**

c.1943, convention badge **$85**

Collector Resources

Clubs

The following clubs or organizations may be of interest to Coca-Cola collectors, some directly like The Coca-Cola Collectors Club, and others indirectly like Can Collectors, and Advertising Collectors Clubs, etc.

Antique Advertising Assoc. of America (AAAA)
P. O. Box 1121
Morton Grove, IL 60053

The Coca-Cola Collectors Club International
P. O. Box 49166
Atlanta, GA 30359

Calendar Collector Society
18222 Flower Hill Way #299
Gaithersburg, MD 20879

Figural Bottle Opener Collectors
Nancy Robb
3 Avenue A
Latrobe, PA 15650

American Matchcover Collecting Club
P. O. Box 18481
Asheville, NC 28814

International Lighter Collectors
P. O. Box 536
Quitman, TX 74783

Publications

Antique Trader
700 East State St.
Iola, WI 54990-0001

Auctions and Appraisers

Nostalgia Publications
Mail Bid Auctions (Soda Pop)
Published twice a year
Write for info.
Allan Petretti
P.O. Box 4175
River Edge, NJ 07661

Just For Openers
John Stanley
3712 Sunningdale Way
Durham, NC 27707

National Association of
Paper and Advertising Collectors
P. O. Box 500
Mount Joy, PA 17552

The Crown Collectors Society Int.
John Vetter
4300 San Juan Dr.
Fairfax, VA 22030

Museums
The World of Coca-Cola
adjacent to underground Atlanta
For information call (404) 676–5151

The Schmidt Museum of
Coca-Cola Memorabilia
Elizabethtown, KY
For information call (502) 737–4000

Bibliography

Allen, Frederick. "Secret Formula." *Harper's Business Weekly*. 1994.

American Soft Drink Journal, *19th Annual Blue Book,* Vol. 104, No. 676. Atlanta: McFadden Business Publications, Spring 1957.

American Soft Drink Journal, *20th Annual Blue Book*, Vol. 106, No. 688. Atlanta: McFadden Business Publications, Spring 1958.

Armstrong, William. *Lillian Nordica's Hints to Singers*. New York: E. P. Dutton & Co., 1922.

Bailey, Joseph W., Attorney for respondents; Koke Company of America (respondents).

Bateman, Bill and Randy Schaeffer. *Coca-Cola Collectibles: The New Compact Study Guide and Identifier*. Edison, New Jersey: Cartwell Books, Inc., 1996.

Bell, Hunter. *History of Coca-Cola* (unpublished). Atlanta: Coca-Cola Company.

Bigham, A. Walker. *The Snake-Oil Syndrome: Patent Medicine Advertising*. Boston: Christopher Publishing House, 1994.

Bowers, Q. David. *The Moxie Encyclopedia*. New York: The Vestal Press, 1985.

Brown, Diva. "The True History of Coca-Cola and My-Coca." *The Southern Carbonator and Bottler*. February 1909.

———. "A Document in Evidence: My-Coca and Its Relation To Coca-Cola." Birmingham: My-Coca Syrup Company. 1912.

Buechner, Harry N. *Norman Rockwell: Artist and Illustrator*. New York: Harry N. Abrams, 1970.

Campbell, William. *Big Beverage*. Atlanta: Tupper & Love, 1952.

Campbell, J. Duncan. *New Belt Buckles of the Old West*. Northfield, Connecticut: Campbell, 1973.

Candler, Howard. *Asa Griggs Candler*. Atlanta: Emory University Press, 1950.

Charles, Barbara Fahs and J.R. Taylor. *Dream of Santa: Haddon Sundblom's Advertising Paintings for Christmas 1931-1964*. New York: Gramercy Books, 1992.

Charles, Elliott. *Mr. Anonymous: Robert Woodruff of Coca-Cola*. Atlanta: Cherokee Publishing, 1982.

Collins, Allan and Drake Elvgren. *Elvgren, His Life and Art*. Portland, Oregon: Collectors Press, 1998.

Cope, Jim. *Soda Water Advertising*. Padukah, Kentucky: Collector Books, 1974.

Clymer, Floyd. *Scrapbook of Early Advertising Art*. New York: Bonanza Books, 1955.

DeCourtivron, Gael. *Coca-Cola Toy Trucks*. Padukah: Collector Books, 1995.

Dietz, Lawrence. "Soda-Pop Art." Supplement to the *Los Angeles Times*, February 9, 1969.

———. *Soda-Pop: The History of Advertising Art and Memorabilia of Soft Drinks in America*. New York: Simon and Schuster, 1973.

Ebner, Steve. *Vintage Coca-Cola Machines.* Middletown, Maryland: Fun-Tronics, 1989.

———. *Vintage Coca-Cola Machines, Vol. II.* Middletown, Maryland: Fun-Tronics, 1996.

Elliott, Charles. *A Biography of The "Boss" Robert Winship Woodruff.* Atlanta: C. Elliott, 1979.

Enes, Bill. *Silent Salesmen, Too.* Lenexa, Kansas: Walsworth, 1995.

Enrico, Roger. *The Other Guy Blinked: How Pepsi Won The Cola Wars.* New York: Bantam, 1986.

Garrett, Franklin. *The Black Book/History of Coca-Cola 1886-1940,* (unpublished). Atlanta: The Coca-Cola Company, 1940.

———. *Coca-Cola: A Chronological History 1886-1962.* Atlanta: The Coca-Cola Company, 1962.

———. "Those Coca-Cola Collectibles." *The Antiques Journal,* No. 7, July 1968.

———. *Atlanta and Environs: A Chronicle of Its People and Events,* Vol. 1 and Vol. II. Atlanta: University of Georgia Press, 1988.

Garrison, Webb. *The Legacy of Atlanta: A Short History.* Atlanta: Peachtree Publishers, 1987.

Goldstein, Shelly and Helen. *Coca-Cola Collectibles,* Vols. 1-4. Woodland Hills, California: Goldstein, 1972-1976.

Graham, Elizabeth Candler. *The Real Ones: Four Generations of the First Family of Coca-Cola.* Fort Lee, New Jersey: Barricade Books, 1992.

Greising, David. *I'd Like The World To Buy A Coke: The Life and Leadership of Roberto Goizueta.* New York: John Wiley & Sons, 1997.

Hake, Ted. *Hake's Guide To TV Collectibles.* Radnor, Pennsylvania: Wallace-Homestead, 1990.

Hasty, Ronald W. and R. Ted Will. *Marketing.* San Francisco: Canfield Press, 1975.

Hazelcorn, Jane and Howard. *Hazelcorn's Price Guide to Tin Vienna Art Plates.* Teaneck, New Jersey: H.J.H. Publications, 1987.

Hecht, Adelaide. *The Great Patent Medicine Era.* New York: Grosslet & Dunlap, 1970.

Hester, R. L. *The Coca-Cola Connection.* Atlanta: Khoka Productions, Inc., 1987.

Hoy, Anne. *Coca-Cola: The First Hundred Years.* Atlanta: The Coca-Cola Company, 1986.

Kahn, E. J., Jr. *The Big Drink: The Story of Coca-Cola.* New York: Random House, 1950.

King, Monroe Martin. *Pharmacy In History.* Atlanta: American Institute of the History of Pharmacy, 1987.

Klug, Ray. *Antique Advertising Encyclopedia,* Vol. I and II. Gas City, Indiana: L-W Book Sales, 1985.

Kurtz, Wilbur. *Catalog of Metal Service Trays and Art Plates.* Atlanta: Archives, The Coca-Cola Company, 1970.

Lippincott, Wilmot. *Outdoor Advertising.* New York: McGraw-Hill, 1923.

Martin, Milward W. *Twelve Full Ounces.* New York: Holt, Rinehart and Winston, 1962.

Mayo, P. Randolph, Jr. *Coca-Cola Heritage: A Photographic History of The Biedenharn Coca-Cola Bottling Business.* Austin, Texas: Mayo, 1990.

Meyer Bros. *Drug Trade Catalog*, Vol. XXIV, No. 2. Meyer Brothers, St. Louis, MO, 1903.

Mix, Richard. *The Mix Guide to Commemorative Bottles*. Atlanta: Mix, 1997.

Munsey, Cecil. "Coca-Cola 'A Refreshing Taste of America'." Reprinted from August/September issues of *Western Collector* magazine, San Francisco, 1967.

———. *The Illustrated Guide to the Collectibles of Coca-Cola*. New York: Hawthorn Books, 1972.

Muzio, Jack. *Collectible Tin Advertising Trays*. Los Angeles: J. Muzio, 1972.

Nostalgia Publications Mail-Bid Auctions, No. 1 through No. 60. Hackensack, New Jersey: Nostalgia Publications, 1976-2006.

Oliver, Thomas. *The Real Coke—The Real Story*. New York: Random House, 1986.

Palazzini, Fiora Steinbach. *Coca-Cola Super Star*. New York: Barron's, 1988.

Pendergrast, Mark. *For God, Country and Coca-Cola*. New York: Charles Scribner's Sons, 1988.

Petretti, Allan. "The Calendar Art of The Coca-Cola Company." *Antique Trade Weekly*, Dubuque, Iowa, April 12, 2000.

Petretti, Allan and Chris Beyer. *Classic Coca-Cola Serving Trays*. Dubuque: Antique Trader Books, 1998.

———. *Classic Coca-Cola Calendars*. Iola, Wisconsin: Antique Trader Books, 1999.

Reno, Dawn E. *Advertising Identification and Price Guide*. New York: Avon Books, 1993.

Riley, John J. A *History of The American Soft Drink Industry*. Washington: American Bottlers of Carbonated Beverages, 1958.

———. *A History of The American Soft Drink Industry*. New York: Arno, 1958. Reprint 1972.

Rowland, Sanders and Bob Terrell. *Papa Coke: Sixty-Five Years Selling Coca-Cola*. Ashville: Bright Mountain Books, 1986.

Schaeffer, Randy and Bill Bateman. *Coca-Cola: A Collectors Guide to New and Vintage Coca-Cola Memorabilia*. Philadelphia: Courage Books, 1995.

Schiff, Joseph L. and Leonard. *Edward Payson Baird: Inventor, Industrialist, Entrepreneur*. New York: Clinton Press, 1975.

Schmidt, Bill and Jan. *The Schmidt Museum Collection of Coca-Cola Memorabilia*. Elizabethtown, Kentucky: Schmidt, 1985.

Shartar, Martin and Norman Shavin. *The Wonderful World of Coca-Cola*. Atlanta: Capricorn Corp., 1981.

Silverman, Milton. *Magic in a Bottle*. New York: MacMillan, 1941.

Strang, Lewis C. *Famous Prima Donnas*. Boston: L.C. Page & Co., 1900.

Taylor, Norman. *Plant Drugs that Changed the World*. London: George Allen & Unwin, 1965.

Tedlow, Richard. *New and Improved: The Story of Mass Marketing in America*. New York: Basic Books, 1990.

Opinions, orders, injunctions and decrees relating to unfair competition and infringement of trademark, Vol. 1 (1923), Vol. 2 (1923-30). Vol. 3 (1931-38). Atlanta: The Coca-Cola Company.

The Coca-Cola Company: An Illustrated Profile. Atlanta: The Coca-Cola Company, 1944.

The Coca-Cola Company: Portrait of a Worldwide Company. The Coca-Cola Company, Atlanta, 1971.

Purity Lives In a House of Glass. The Coca-Cola Company, Atlanta, 1954.

Chronological History of The Coca-Cola Company, 1886 to 1969. Atlanta: The Coca-Cola Company, 1969.

The Chronicle of Coca-Cola Since 1886. Atlanta: The Public Relations Dept. of The Coca-Cola Company, 1973.

The Romance of Coca-Cola. Atlanta: The Coca-Cola Company, 1916.

This Is Your Company. Atlanta: The Coca-Cola Company, 1966.

The Coca-Cola Bottler (50th Anniversary Issue) Vol. LI, No. I. Atlanta: The Coca-Cola Company, April 1959.

Third Affidavit of Samuel C. Dobbs, June 7, 1920, District Court of The United States for the District of Delaware. The Coca-Cola Bottling Company (complainant) vs. The Coca-Cola Company (defendant). Atlanta: The Coca-Cola Company, 1920.

The American Way of Business. Atlanta: The Coca-Cola Company, 1967.

The Next Station Will Be. . . An Album of photographs of Railroad Depots, Vol. I through Vol. V. Rahway, New Jersey: Railroadians of America, 1973-1977.

Turner, E. S. *The Shocking History of Advertising.* London: Michael Joseph, 1952.

Walters, Jeff. *The Complete Guide to Collectible Picnic Coolers & Ice Chests.* Pollock Pines, California: Memory Lane, 1994.

———. *Classic Soda Machines.* Pollock Pines, California: Memory Lane, 1992.

———. *Classic Soda Machines*, Second Edition. Pollock Pines, California: Memory Lane, 1995.

Watters, Pat. *Coca-Cola: An Illustrated History.* New York: Doubleday, 1978.

Weinberger, Marty and Don. *Coca-Cola Trays from Mexico and Canada.* Willow Grove, Pennsylvania: Weinberger, 1979.

Whitehill, Bruce. *Games: American Boxed Games and Their Makers, 1822-1992.* Radnor, Pennsylvania: Wallace-Homestead, 1992.

Witzel, Gyvel Young and Michael Karl. *Soda Pop: From Miracle Medicine to Pop Culture.* Stillwater, Minnesota: Town Square Books, 1998.

Yazijian, Harvey, and Louis, J. C. *The Cola Wars.* New York: Everest House, 1980.

Index

Index